MY HUSBAND
HAS DIED, BUT THAT'S NOT
THE FUNNY PART

MY HUSBAND
HAS DIED, BUT THAT'S NOT
THE FUNNY PART

*When laughter and love overcome
grief and loss*

Debra J. Blood

authorHOUSE®

AuthorHouse™
1663 Liberty Drive
Bloomington, IN 47403
www.authorhouse.com
Phone: 1-800-839-8640

Published by AuthorHouse   02/15/2013

ISBN: 978-1-4817-1667-3 (sc)
ISBN: 978-1-4817-1666-6 (e)

Library of Congress Control Number: 2013902845

This book is dedicated to:

God

For letting me hear "I am with you" when I needed it the most

*For **Timothy David** and **Sarah Jane***

When death comes to call, and it will, may you answer that call with dignity, strength, grace and mostly laughter

You are mine and Dennis' pride & joy

I love you forever, Mom

For **My Parents, Duward & Ramona**

Without you I would have never known the way

*For so many **friends & family** who not **only lifted us up***
during the darkest days but are still holding us up today, I will be forever grateful

From the bottom of my heart thank you all for taking this journey with me

For **Dennis**

This is for you

May the world now know the precious soul you were

I pray you know that I kept my promise

As you did yours

Until I hold you again

Debra

SPECIAL DEDICATION,
"FOR YOU, AUNT ELAINE"

In every life there are basic needs or desires within each beating heart. We all want to be heard, understood, and accepted for who we are, respected, admired and above all else "loved." Dennis was no different. From a small child to the man he became he was seeking the same things that we all do. He found each of these needs met within the arms of his wife and children, where most would expect. He however also found all of this in the heart of a woman he called "Aunt."

As I took this journey with each word, each tear soaked stroke of the keyboard, each giggle over a memory I now hold closer to me than anything I can touch, I was shown so many blessings. They came in the form of new friends, renewal of old friendships, someone saying "you gave me hope today", seeing my own children come through this storm with a smile and with such character that I know Dennis is "beaming with pride" through the clouds.

I received so much support over the past year. So many uplifting words of encouragement from people I have loved for years and those I just recently met, to those I only know from our online exchanges. But this message I am about to share with you was different. This was someone who "loved him too". This was special. It struck the very heart of what I was trying to say, it let me know that my efforts to honor this man were not in vain, that someone really understood what I was trying to achieve each time I wrote, "Dear Dennis".

This message was from Dennis' Aunt Elaine who lives in Buffalo, N.Y. He loved her heart and soul, as she did him. Each business trip to Cleveland resulted in a side trip to see Aunt Elaine and Uncle Britt. He laughed like a kid when he came home and proudly proclaimed, "My Aunt did my laundry while I stayed with her (giggle) because she loves me Debra!" She stayed up till' the early hours of the night hearing every story he had to tell, sharing his worries, his hopes for his future, and his love for the kids as he told her with pride of "the latest adventures of Timmy and Sarah." They loved to golf and so this they often shared. His Uncle was very knowledgeable in the same areas of interest that Dennis was so he admired his Uncle and loved to talk to him about things only they seem to understand. He was their *son*, they were his *parents,* voids were filled as he lost his sweet mother years earlier and he was sadly estranged from his father. When I came into his life with all the baggage and issues of my divorce they never once ever made me or my children feel like anything but "family". We stayed in their home, we ate at their table, we gathered at their house for reunions big and small. As I waded through this year of grief I did my best to stay in touch as I believed with all my heart Dennis would appreciate nothing more than for me to remain close to this part of his family. As I wrote I shared some of my posts and stories with Aunt Elaine. I wanted her to know how very much I loved her nephew and how my heart ached for him. What you are about to read from someone who knew and loved Dennis as I did, means more to me than I can explain. In some way that you may not completely understand, to me this says "*I kept my promise.*"

Debra:

He had such a short life and I asked our Lord "why". I wondered if he was happy. I've prayed for an answer, knowing that this is something we "just learn to accept." And then, I read your messages to Dennis. I reread them again, shared them with Uncle. We talked about those messages, shared our favorite memories. I read them again . . . and then I realized . . . without a doubt, Dennis was happy and relished his life with you and the kids. It was his purpose. It was his journey in this life. There was my answer in each and every message filled with the love and humor that was just so Dennis. It was made possible by you. You recreated all those moments for us. He had you to hold steady, a purpose in life. With each and every message, you pay tribute to his memory and let each one of us know and feel once again, the wonderful man that he was. So, as I wrote to you so many months ago . . . For the love and joy you brought to his life, we love you. And today we add . . . . For the honor you bring to his memory, may the Lord Bless you.

Auntie E

CONTENTS

SIDE BY SIDE

(About the cover photo)

We moved to Easley, (Greenville) South Carolina in January 2006. Moving from Florida where most things were flat and not so lush, we just loved the mountains, the changing of the leaves in the fall and the wildlife of the Carolinas. The first year here as the colors changed Dennis and I just fell in love with the "Japanese maple" tree that stands just off the sidewalk where the garage meets the house. This tree would go from various shades of green to the most beautiful deep reds that you have ever seen and he would frequently talk about how much he loved having it in our yard.

On 9/25/2011 when God called Dennis home, ironically enough it was beneath this very tree that he adored that I found him lying. It was an otherwise beautiful sunshiny day of fall and the tree was nearing its fullest beauty. It has been said to me that "if this was the last thing he had seen that day" then we should be thankful for the view that God had provided.

One year later, mid-October, I took my IPAD outside on another similar bright day to capture some of the breathtaking colors of fall. I love pictures, picture taking, and I love leaves so this is something I do "just for fun." I am not sure what made me walk over to "Dennis' tree" that day but I did. I usually did everything I could to avoid that specific area as not to provoke unnecessary painful memories of just a year prior. But this day, I did not stop. I walked up under the tree, trying to place myself where he would have been. I thought, "if this was the last thing you saw that day Dennis, I want to know what that looked like."

Standing where he would have been, I angled my camera on my IPAD just so as to avoid direct sun, and then I looked straight up in the direction of heaven where I believe him to be resting. There it was . . . ***only two*** . . . only two red leaves out of a tree of green. Side by side . . . one for him . . . one for me.

FOREWORD

My mother has been a widow since 1988. She has lived all of these years without her best friend, her confidant, her "world", my Dad. They, Duward & Ramona or Duie & Monie, as they were affectionately known to friends and family were blessed with nearly 28 years together come 9/20/1988; that was the day God called my father home. We (Dennis & Debra) were blessed with nearly 16 years come 9/25/2011, when God called again and this time, my best friend, my confidant, my "world", my husband Dennis, answered the call.

The day our father passed all those years ago, my brother and I both believed that our lives had changed forever. We believed that we would need to "care for" our mother, after all she was 67 and to us that meant "elderly", right? (Just to prove us wrong, as I write this she is in my laundry room working her magic with stain remover at the spry young age of 91. Go Mom!)

We thought it was up to us to be there to help her make decisions. Ensure that she was not taken advantage of by any evil that lurked out there in this big world. Make sure she still got out and took part in activities that kept her active and young, handle paperwork and bills, manage her healthcare and not let the loneliness of losing Dad overtake her as the days went on. In our eyes he had been the decision-maker. He was the one who "knew what to do", he was the one who spoke for the family and she added her two cents in private, followed by supporting "his" decision as "theirs" as a woman of her generation was raised to do. What we didn't know, what we had no way to foresee, was while we thought Dad was the strong one and she respectfully the poster child for "stand by your man", we soon learned that his strength may just have been in part due to the woman he so lovingly referred to as "Mother" for all of those years. Let me take you back to 1988 for just a moment.

Mom and Dad had convinced me at the young age of 22 years to leave our home state of Michigan and come live with them in south Florida. As Dad said, "where the sun shines every day and you can get to the ocean in just a blink or two" (my father, always the salesman). My parents were "older" parents. I was born when Dad was 47 years old, and Mom 43 years old, this being his second marriage and her first. By 1988 they were respectively "retirees" living in the south, watching the oranges grow, never missing a shuttle launch ("Deb we can see it from our front yard! Can't do THAT in Michigan!"), attending church, driving to town for lunch, bragging to the folks "back home" about the weather, and just loving their life of leisure. One of the biggest reasons they left the cold tundra of Michigan to spend their golden years in Florida was that Dad had a "bad leg". This meant that he suffered an illness in his early years that left him walking with a limp for his entire life. According to Dad this was not "all bad" as this leg earned him his honorary meteorologist certification as "I can tell it's going to rain today Deb, I can feel it in my bones!" His right leg never wanted to bend at the hip very well so upon arrival in Florida they sold the family wagon and bought a Cadillac. It was silver, it was way more car than they needed however the biggest selling point was that it had the room for Dad to extend his leg in front of him while, the "Queen Mum" (i.e. Mom) "chauffeured" him around in style.

When my argument that all residents of Florida had gray hair and only ate oranges ran its course, I gave in to my Dad's pleadings and moved to Florida in 1986. I secured a job as a 911 Dispatcher for the ambulance service (one of the coolest jobs I ever had let me add). I was working this job when my Dad passed. Prior to his passing about once every week or so I would get a call at work from Mom asking if it would be ok if they stopped by work to pick me up and take me to lunch. Of course it was, and those were some of the best memories I have of them during those years. We talked of the "emergency" calls I had taken that morning and we would match the "facts" with what Mom had picked up by listening to the scanner she had purchased just to hear "her girl" at work each day.

After Dad had passed, maybe 2-3 weeks had gone by and I was at work. The phone rang and it was Mom. She asked the familiar question of "was it ok" and "did I want to go to lunch". Nothing unusual about the request other than this was the first time Dad would not be with us. I showed some concern as to if she really wanted to do this. It seemed so "early" for her to be getting out, (always the protector I was) but she assured me it was fine and she would be there soon and I should come out to the parking lot to meet her.

Do you remember the commercial slogan "it's not your father's Oldsmobile?" Well, I walked out to the parking lot, Mom was there waving at me with a "let's go." I took a few steps in her direction and then it hit me . . . Where was the Cadillac? Those being my exact words, my mother pointed to a white Cutlass Calais just past where she was standing. I said, "That's nice Mom but really . . . where is your car?" She pointed to the smaller white car again and smiled very big and very proud. Oh my gosh, she did not. Yes she certainly did. Mom said, "You know Deb, we had that Cadillac for your Dad, it was because of his leg and his need for room but I don't need that, so I drove myself to the dealership, picked out a car, traded in the Cadillac and here it is!" She ended that with . . . "Deb, it's not your father's Oldsmobile; it's your Mother's!" (She was pretty proud of herself for that one.) It was at that very moment that I knew my brother and I were way off. We could stand down for just a while, no need to put a down payment on "Shady Pines" just yet. The woman who had stood behind Dad all of those years was now walking out in front. She was not weak, she did not need us to "care for" her (not just yet anyway) and her .02 cents was probably more like .20 and Dad loved her for that very reason. She was strong, she held her head high, and with a grace all her own she moved forward with the full intent of honoring his memory and their love . . . ***in her own way***. What I truly had no way of knowing then was that I was being shown the example of how to carry yourself, how to persevere in the face of tragedy and heartache, as 23 years later, almost to the day, it would become my turn.

Now allow me to fast-forward to the year 2011. Not a person alive (ok maybe one or two) does not know of, nor is not a member of an online social network. We all have over 500 friends' right? We post each day, we mark our every move, whom we are dating, how we "feel" at any given moment, what our cute kids said and "here is picture of them while they said it", the current events of the day and our righteous opinion given of said events. How we feel about our job, showing our support for our military, lifting each other up, cheering each other on, talking of whether we were "Team Edward" or "Team Jacob" even though us "40 something's" were way too old to be making that call. Who we think the world should vote for (this year it was Obama vs. Romney), and please trust me when I say, it's "safer" to discuss your vote for "Jacob vs. Edward". How much weight we lost "this week" and what brand of seaweed we ate in a shake each morning to get to that weight. It's crazy but it's the world today. I am not going to lie; I am the "Queen" of posting. Before 9/25/2011, I posted just as much as my friends did and probably more. (Ok friends, hush, I know what you are thinking!) I shared a billion pictures and thoughts. I enjoyed more than anything the precious gift of being able to reach out and communicate daily with those that I have loved over the years but have not seen since high school or three jobs back, and the new friends I have made along the way.

When my world came crashing down on 9/25/2011, I didn't go out and buy a Calais like my Mother. I did however, ironically enough, purchase my husband's work vehicle. About a week after he passed I climbed into the car to make a quick trip to the store when I realized that I could strongly feel him with me whereas, I had this feeling nowhere else. To me he was gone, and that hollow, empty void was one like no other. Yet there was an overwhelming sense of comfort when I would get in and shut the door that I could not explain; maybe it was that he spent so much time every day in this car, but it was truly as if he was there with me. Whatever the reason it was a leased fleet car and it was up for option to purchase in just a few months and Dennis had said he wanted me to have it then. I called his Manager and asked him "How do I purchase Dennis' car—I don't want to let it go?" I walked through the steps to purchase, register, license, etc. It now is in my driveway bringing me comfort still to this day.

The world is so different than it was in 1988. When my best friend left me, I needed an outlet. I needed to scream, yell, cry and just get it out. I needed to tell the world of this beautiful man that had my heart. Mom had my brother and I, little pieces of my father to remain here with her and be a daily reminder of his strength, humor, and never ending need to "invent" something and tell the world the way it should be. I however, did not have Dennis' children. God did not bless us in this way. HE did however bless us with Timothy and Sarah. These were the two step-children that

Dennis loved and raised when he "didn't have to". Everything Dennis did everyday he did for "us". I wanted everyone to know what this horrific grief felt like as I was certain I would not emerge from underneath the so-called rubble that had fallen on our family. I had such an overwhelming need to express how much I loved him and what he meant to his family and this world. I was determined that he not be forgotten.

I needed human contact but I live in Easley, S.C. in a small community and none of my friends and family is nearby. So, I did what a woman of "today" would do. I posted my feelings daily. Sometimes in the beginning more than once (you will see) in a day. I told stories as the memories flooded in. I gave updates as to how the roller coaster ride of grief was going and most importantly to the benefit of my sanity I wrote to my husband ("Dear Dennis") as if he could read my posts from heaven. I used this as therapy. I had to get it out. They say, "Let go and Let God", well sometimes that is the most difficult thing to do as how could I ever think of letting him go? So I wrote, I cried, I wrote more, I laughed, I cried more . . . I used this as a means to an end for my severely broken heart.

Each love is special, each life is precious, each loss is deep and mine is no more tragic than one that you may have experienced or God forbid will experience one day. It is my hope that in these pages you will smile with me through the tears as we walk back through the life and love that was "Dennis and Debra". It is my intent that as you read the stories of what made us who we were and as you then step with me through the dark days since his passing, this will somehow give you hope that *love and laughter really can overcome grief.*

I know you may not know us personally. That's ok, we were nobody special. We were just like you and your husband or wife. We were "just a guy from Buffalo who fell in love with a girl from Michigan." We were two hearts that joined as one. We were young, full of life and bound together with a twine that only God could weave. We said "till' death do us part" but unfortunately we never truly knew how soon that would be. God had a plan. It was not ours.

I write this book for my children and even for my grandchildren that I may never know. I write this book for Dennis to say "I could not have been prouder to be your wife and I will never forget you." I write this book for myself, as the money I have saved in therapy, and the healing of my broken heart has been nothing short of amazing.

I write this book for you! It is my wish that by sharing my grief of losing this sweet man you will know you are not alone in your grief that you have felt or again, unfortunately will know someday as we all do.

You may not have lost a close loved one and know this grief that I speak of, or maybe you have been there like me and know it all too well and will see yourself in my words. Either way the thing about grief that we all come to know eventually . . . you were not the only one who felt that way, you will be mad, maybe at yourself, maybe at your deceased loved one and yes, even maybe at God. You will cry a river of tears, the days immediately following, the weeks to come and yes even a year or years later as you mourn this loss. You will be devastated and fight to hang on to what was very much "your world" but now is slowly becoming a "part of your past". You will laugh (I promise) and at the most inopportune moments. You will find yourself reaching out to help others that have suffered a loss because now you are a member of the "club" too, and trust me the dues to enter are high. You will believe you are a million steps ahead of the game only to suddenly find you are thrown right back to the day it all happened. Even though you may have told your children, as most of us have, "nobody said life is fair", you will ignore your own wise words and declare life completely "unfair". You will make decisions that you never ever thought you would have to make. You will go to dark places that you never knew existed in your mind. You will pick up the Bible because now you "must" know where they went and if they are ok. You will summon a strength that only God knew you had all along. You will meet a new you and find out really what you are made of, and who your friends really are. You will grow in your faith without even knowing it is happening, you will "let go and let God" and it will be ok when you do. You will find love again and you will find a reason to put one foot in front of the other. You will come to remember "them" with a smile and not always a tear, and when they say "time heals all wounds" . . . you will want to locate and break every clock in the house as you wait for each painful second to pass. Hopefully you will come to understand that their death and even ours is not truly the end, and the love and life we all share is a gift from God and should be celebrated.

Like my mother before me who showed me how to move forward in the face of death, I pray that this reflection of a love and life gone too soon will show my children the same grace and courage but only from a different more modern view.

Walk with me through this year following the passing of my sweet husband Dennis, and if you take away anything from our story, it is my prayer simply . . . that you will.

SAYING GOOD-BYE

Dennis James Bujanowski

6/10/1965-9/25/2011

I didn't want to go through those emergency room doors, but the ambulance driver seemed to keep pulling me that way. It was as if his job wasn't quite done until he had delivered not only you on the stretcher, but me as well to that little stark room where you hear them say "I am sorry ma'am but we did all that we could do."

I knew what was coming. I heard them call for the Chaplin and a social services worker; I was not ignorant to the ways of a hospital. I worked for years as a secretary in an emergency room in south Florida, I used to be an EMT and a 911 Dispatcher and I have witnessed those words being said to more than one person. I remember cringing as a very young woman wailed in pain and slid down the side of a counter as they gently told her that her young seemingly strong husband was not coming home with her that day. He had died during drills at the local Air Force Bombing Range. I watched as a man in his 80's was told that the woman he had spent the last 50 years with was now in a "better place". He said between quiet sobs, "But how am I to go on without her, she was my best friend?" I wanted to run out of that hospital that night and hold his hand as his tears fell and hear every story they ever had to tell.

I watched it happen to other people and my heart would always break into a million pieces, but I didn't really know what they were feeling, where that scream came from in that woman or how that elderly man must have really felt going through those doors alone that only hours earlier he had entered with "her." I didn't really know until those words were said to me.

I didn't really know until they said the love of my life, Dennis James Bujanowski . . . **was gone.**

1

They told me I could come in and spend as much time as I needed with you to say "good-bye".

Good-bye? Didn't we just meet? Wasn't it just last week when you yelled "I love you" in the Taco Bell drive-thru? It seems like yesterday that you called me on the phone and all I heard was Bob Seger singing, "Someday lady you'll accompany me". Wasn't our first kiss that made my knees go weak just months ago, our wedding in which I cried trying to say my vows with Alabama singing "There's no way I could make it without you" in the background.

The trip to the house on the river in N.C. where you fished for trout during the day with Tim while I tried new recipes. At night we settled in front of a glowing fire and just cuddled in silence on the couch as no words needed to be said, that was just last month right? All of those trips to Buffalo to see the kids, the Nascar races cheering on Dale, Sr., the Super Bowl parties we hosted and suffered for being Buffalo Bills fans. Your first trip to Fisher Lake (Three Rivers, MI) where you shared my childhood memories and met my lifelong friends was just this past summer. Our first night in our new South Carolina home with only a cooler and an air mattress, you and Sarah going down Sliding Rock, you and Tim fishing at Mills River, the excitement at the birth of all our puppies, the complete heartache we shared the day we lost what would have been our daughter before this soul ever had a chance, the hug we shared on your birthday 6/10/2008 when the Judge said the kids were coming home with us to live, no, wasn't that all just yesterday?

How could it possibly be time to say good-bye Dennis? How could this be?

I laid my head on your chest. *I promised you I would make you proud and would honor your memory* and I thanked you as I knew each day everything you did whispered "I love you Debra". Every decision you made was done out of your love for me, Timothy and Sarah. I thanked you for being the father that you didn't have to be. I thanked you for the happiest moments of my life, and for showing me more love than anyone has ever done. I held your hand as I told you how very sorry I was that I could not save you that day. I asked you to forgive me as I tried so hard but all of my efforts, tears and love would just not bring you back. It's true what they say . . . if love alone could save you.

I told you that had I known this morning when we woke that this would be our last day on earth together, I would have held you in my arms until the final moment came so you didn't truly have to go alone. I asked you if you were with your Mom, your Grandma, and others that passed before you. I prayed as I held my face against yours and told God that you were so very special and your heart was so good and full of love.

God heard me say if I could not take care of you as I had done each day for nearly the last 16 years, I begged God to keep you until we could be together again. I asked you to be there for me when I arrived no matter how many more miles were left in my journey.

I kissed your forehead and your lips one last time, I caressed your face. I did what I never thought I would ever have to do . . . alone . . . I said good-bye.

READ THE INSTRUCTIONS

When you are young, with all the pure innocence that God made you with, you believe that life will go on forever and there will always be a tomorrow. When you are middle-aged you start to realize that tomorrow may not be promised and time is the one thing you really cannot control, slow down or grasp in your hands. When you lose someone you love suddenly, you know for a fact that nothing will be the same again and life is never what it seems.

Maybe the first thing you need to know about us is that we both came with our own specific viewpoints on life like so many other couples. We were the true definition of "opposites attract". Dennis saw everything black and white. He did not trust easily or let others in quickly. He just accepted that life was not always fair, you only got what you earned and worked hard for and as he simply stated so many times, "it is what it is Debra". I on the other hand had a much "rosier" viewpoint in that I believed you trusted and loved wide open until someone gave you a reason to feel otherwise. I believed there was good in everyone and all you had to do was take "5 minutes and a cup of coffee" and surely you would find it. I laughed easily, loved without hesitation and as he loved to say, "Debra you just want to hold hands and teach the world to sing". Yes, yes I do.

We talked about death and dying before of course. After all Dennis and I had both lost a parent unexpectedly and other loved ones and we knew what loss felt like and what it did to a family. What we hadn't experienced or could not prepare for was losing the other half of our heart in an instant.

Dennis had family members that shared his heart condition and he lost them also at what would be considered "too young". So we talked about dying, death, loss and the "What ifs" of the world way too frequently. Even while the intelligent part of you knows it is going to happen "someday", you can't stop it. The part of you that has the ability to protect your heart by making you live in denial says this is something you don't have to think about for a very long time to come . . . "so don't."

Between 2001-2005 we lived in Oceanway (North Jacksonville, FL) on our new property that held a mobile home and garage on three beautiful tree covered acres. We shared some of the best times of our lives together at this address. We moved here to get away from living "on top of our neighbors". It was heaven on earth to us and we had never been happier. In 2003 we became man and wife and while living in this home some of my best memories surrounded "my birthday."

It was my birthday, November 16, and I was always excited about that day because of one reason . . . Dennis. He never failed to make it special. He always remembered my love for crab legs and ensured a big dinner out or in but the menu was always the same. I was not a drinker by any means as alcohol triggered migraines in me but every year on my birthday, he would buy me a fifth of tequila and we would do shots, listen to music and have some of the best times we ever had. It became a strange tradition of sorts and one year it included our best friends from down the road, a video camera, a cowboy hat and me trying to "two-step" to Bon Jovi. Oh dear Lord, it was the night that the phrase "I love you more than life itself" came to be. Tell me you haven't been there. Tell me you haven't had a little too much to drink and started to "love everyone heart and soul and became overcome with an endless desire to proclaim this to the world." I swore if I had thought of it I would have taken that video to the funeral home and had it tossed in with Dennis at the time of his cremation.

One particular birthday stands out however but not so much with a smile. Dennis would be what you consider a "private" person. He only shared his true feelings and thoughts with me, yet he would go to any length to protect me from being hurt, even if it meant "not telling me". He came home to me this November day and again I was excited as it was my birthday and I knew the evening was going to be filled with so much fun, laughter and sweet moments with my guy. The look on his face when he came through the door immediately worried me and my uneasiness did not dissipate any when he motioned me to the back porch and said, "come out here, we need to talk".

He started with "I don't want you to get upset". Well please . . . tell me who says that to you and you respond by **not** getting upset? My thoughts ran wild in my head at lightning speed. If there was ever anything I knew about my husband it was that first he was an excellent provider and second he would never ever ever be unfaithful to me. So, why I started with my incessive nervous immediate questioning of, "Oh my God, did you lose your job? Are you kidding me, we just moved here and took on this mortgage, what are we going to do without your job?" He might have gotten in a "Debra, no I didn't lose my job" just before I launched into "Is there someone else? I promise you I will hurl you off this porch in twenty seconds or less and all of your belongings if you are getting ready to tell me that you fooled around on me . . . . blah . . . blah . . . blah." Louder and more stern now I got from him, "Debra !!! Calm down you know I would never fool around on you, I love you . . . and I am still employed, but I have to tell you something and if you would just be quiet for two seconds and listen!"

Ok, "be quiet and listen" has never been two of my greatest qualities. However since I had ruled out my two biggest fears I grabbed the arms of the chair I was in tightly, I closed my mouth (extremely rare occurrence), nodded my approval for him to proceed and I waited for the other shoe to drop. Well drop it did.

Dennis began to explain that he had been to the Doctor that day. Doctor? I didn't know he had an appointment with any Doctor? Why did he go to a Doctor and not tell me? After all we knew everything about each other, there were no secrets, and we spent every waking minute together and knew each other more than any two people could.

When I heard the words . . . "Debra I have not been feeling good lately and a couple of times my chest has felt funny and tight . . . ." What? You are having chest pains? How could you have chest pains and not tell me? "Debra, I went to a cardiologist and apparently I have A-Fib like my mother and my uncle did." Ok, WOW! A-Fib is a common cardiac arrhythmia and while many people live with this their entire lives it was the mention of his "mother and his uncle" that put the fear of God into me at that very moment. Dennis' Uncle Tom had passed at the age of 46 years old (same age I lost Dennis) and then his mother died suddenly in 1998. I can't be sure about his Uncle but his mother was also believed to have had A-fib we were told, so what should have been a calm reaction instantly brought panic and tears. He made every attempt to explain that the Doctor had put him on medication and assured him that he was otherwise "healthy" and fine but he needed frequent checkups and had to take this seriously especially due to his family history. While I apologized for the "hurl you off the porch" comment later, in the bottom of my stomach I was almost certain I would have rather heard that there was "another woman" than to have this looming over what was our wonderful life together. I knew what to do about "another woman" (kill her—it all seemed simple), but this . . . I had no control over this. No control = Fear in my world.

So now you know "why" we had the "what if" conversations so often, and when we did it was always very one-sided. If Dennis were to survive me he had "one" plan and that involved a "Spanish maid" (funny man). Why did he always make this joke and not give the serious response? Because first, no one needed to tell him what to do to survive it was "what he did", he wrote the book on how to get things done and live through the worst of times. Then second, the thought never ever crossed his mind that it wouldn't be him going before me. He always told me he would "never make it to 50", and he missed it by 4 years. God I hated how he was "always right" about things.

Turning the tables to the plan initiated when Debra survived Dennis, well . . . bet your bottom dollar it was as long and detailed as any good plan could be. He discussed life insurance, paying off the house, any debt (there was none—thank you Dennis), what to do with his things in the garage, how to handle my retirement, the kid's college, etc. Yes it was a step by step, instruction manual for "how Debra is to live without Dennis". It was all very neatly laid out, it was all very well-orchestrated and *in reality* it went like clockwork and left us secure and safe which was his intent all along.

That was him, the "man with the plan", the guy in charge, the one that had it all figured out and had all the answers. What he didn't tell me was what I was supposed

to do about my broken heart. No, he never gave me a plan for that other than . . .
"you are the loving and happy one Debra, you will meet someone in no time and love
again." Really? Is that how it goes? Just be happy and wa-la a wonderful man pops
into your life and I begin again? There was a reason Dennis handled the logical side
of things and I was President and CEO of "matters of the heart". No, he never told
me how to stop the tears, how to wake up and reach for him in the middle of the night
for the 100th time and not become hysterical. He never prepared me for walking into
a grocery store, seeing his favorite kind of ice cream and losing it in the frozen foods
section. He never said that I would be holding back crocodile tears when I should
have otherwise been smiling as our son graduated high school and basic training or
our daughter went to prom and her own graduation and he wasn't there to see it. He
may have had all the answers to the important "administrative duties" (as he called
them) in life but he could not counsel me of how to breathe without him in my arms
at the end of each day. He took care of us like nobody ever could. For that we are
all forever grateful and proud, but what he just failed to tell me was how I supposed
to love a man like him, consider him my "entire world" and then somehow move
forward to consider him "a part of my past".

This past year has been something that I never thought I would live through let alone
even have to consider happening to me. While I always knew, for all reasons stated
above, that it was a possibility I just chose to remain in my optimistic world (holding
hands and singing) and believe that modern medicine and new technology would
make it all ok. I believed that there was no way God would let us go through all that
we had to bring us to the point of finding each other, sharing a love like no other and
then one beautiful fall day take it all away.

I am thankful for his "instruction manual" and when the roof needed fixing, the
mortgage needed paying, the dishwasher and washing machine broke down (on
the same day) I just flipped through the pages of my manual entitled "What would
Dennis do" and took immediate and decisive action.

My job as I see it now is to write the pages of the "instruction manual" that Dennis
left out. The part that is my area of expertise. The "matters of the heart" directives if
you will. I would never say, "I won't live to be 50" but I will say that when death comes
knocking at the door and this time it's me who answers, I want my children to know
which chapter of the manual to read **first**.

SEPTEMBER 2011

(Facebook daily posts)

"Why?"

9/25/2011:

Today I lost my husband, my best friend, and the love of my life. Today my heart is shattered into a billion pieces. I will love you until the day I die Dennis Bujanowski, you are now and will forever be my only love. I pray that you are resting in the arms of Jesus, and your Mom is by your side. I will be strong and make you proud. I promise.

9/27/2011:

Dear Dennis:

Each morning I open my eyes to this profound heaviness in my chest, this incredible sadness that washes over me as I realized that "yes this is real, and no you are not coming back." I am trying to be strong, but the missing you and shock of it all seems to zap me at times and make me non-functional. My heart is so broken.

9/27/2011:

Dear Dennis:

Today I wore your "sexy lounge pants". Remember you said, "men don't wear pajamas Debra!" I wore your big long soft t-shirt, I called your voicemail to just hear your voice, I look at your picture, I make the calls, and I make the small decisions because big ones are on a 6 month restriction. I keep watching the clock wanting time to just speed up so the pain will stop. I know this is going to get better day by day and for all of our friends and family sending prayers, love and support I am forever grateful.

9/28/2011:

Babe:

It's 3 a.m. and I am awake, missing you, trying not to cry because sometimes when you start it's hard to stop. The world just does not seem right without you in it but I am doing my best to keep things in line and as close to "normal" as possible for the kids. They have been SO good bless their hearts. My brothers are coming this weekend, and your friends are coming to finish the work on the gutters that you were working on when you passed. I am so grateful.

9/28/2011:

Dear Dennis:

Kids needed one more day. They will go back to school tomorrow. I want them to be ok, because I know when they get there other kids (meaning well) may bombard them with statements and questions, as kids would do, and it might be overwhelming. They have a friend in the school nurse and I have made all of their teachers aware. I pray this goes well.

9/29/2011:

Dear Dennis:

I wait for the phone to ring knowing they are going to say I can come get you. I dread that call yet I want you with me so bad I wish it would come sooner. Dennis everyone is showing so much love and support and "your son" Tim is being such a young man and making you so proud. Sarah has not left my side. There are these moments I don't want to move forward and then I hear you say, "it is what it is Debra". ha. Rest my love and send us your strength if you can . . . we love you so.

9/30/2011:

Dear Dennis:

Today I did the hardest thing I have EVER had to do in my life since saying good-bye to you just 5 days ago. Today they handed me the remains of my husband, my best friend, my lover, my protector, my confidant, my life. With my brother at my side we brought you home. I still am in shock, my head spins, waves of pain wash over me and I burst into tears at any given moment. I just keep stepping through each minute of the day praying you and God are both walking by my side.

9/30/2011:

Dear Dennis:

Where there is grief there is humor (This is where you would say, "You are a nerd Debra Blood"). When at the funeral home, my brother Dave put you (in your temporary urn) in the back seat of the car. He STRAPPED YOU IN WITH THE SEATBELT . . . that made us giggle just a little and was the cause of just a few smart comments that I know you would have so appreciated.

NO MOM, YOU DIDN'T
KILL THE FISH

He was long, black, ugly, scaly, big lips protruded from his scary face and he stuck to the side of the fish tank so we could all get a clear shot of his tonsils. He survived two moves, the heat shutting down making the water plunge to sub-zero temps while we were on vacation, yet he thawed and lived to survive me forgetting to feed him when Dennis went away for business. Somewhere around the day before Dennis returned home he said to me on our nightly call, "Have you been feeding the fish?" After the long pause on my end all you could hear from my husband was a fearful and stern, "Debraaaaaaaaaaaaaaaaa". Oops!

His official name was a plecostomus. He was one of the most common and aggressive algae feeders. They have been known to grow up to twenty inches long and can live for years. In our home, he was called by his given name, **"Mr. Al G. Fish."**

I didn't like him, the fish that is. I always called him funny names and was quick to complain about how his upkeep affected our budget and his general lack of purpose in our life. I would walk by the tank pointing at his lips stuck to the glass and announce, "You SUCK!" to which more times than not this made only me laugh. Every person that had ever entered our house would listen as my husband proudly told them that this fish had lived "X" number of years and had survived everything short of WWII. He lived for 16 years, which I am not sure what that is in "fish years" but he outlived my husband by only days. He was the nastiest algae eating fish I had ever seen and when he died, so close after losing Dennis, I did what any person who hated fish would do . . . I cried my eyes out. Mr. Al G. Fish had passed away.

It's a 55-gallon fish tank. It's pretty if you like fish tanks, I never have. I have never liked fish. I don't like fish in a tank, on a plate, in a pan, said Deb I am. I officially claim to be "fish abused" but have never sought counseling for this affliction. I grew up on a lake in southwest Michigan for those not "in the know" and each night, after dinner before the sun went down, my parents would get into their boat with their fishing poles and worms and head just a little ways off shore. Dad said the fishing was best that time of day, I always thought it was so they could get away and talk about us kids and how we were driving them to "fish" and say things like "what were we thinking?" Either way, as the bounty rolled in, we were served a steady diet of fish. There were perch, pike, bass, bluegills and sunfish. You could have it baked, pan-fried, seared, broiled, in butter, on a grill, you name it we ate it. I personally felt deep down in my gills this was bordering on "abuse".

Now my husband, he came from a different "school" of thinking. He loved fish. He loved to fish. He loved the waders, the streams, the worms, the smell, the slime, reeling them in, the net, the challenge and conquest of it all, the stories and pictures. He loved the fish dinner where he would go to Jacksonville to buy fresh haddock and bring it home to South Carolina. He then would dip each filet into a batter made of 1 egg and 1 St. Pauli Girl beer, because "Debra this is the *only* beer that will work". Then you dipped the fish into House of Autry fish breading and proceeded to deep-fry them. This was his "Friday Fish Fry" that he missed from his Buffalo NY childhood.

He kept them as pets, read about them, talked about them, bought house décor with fish on it, visited them at the pet store every chance he got even though I was always in tow advising him that "if it doesn't have fur it can't be a pet". He would have me stand in front of a tank at the store with 30 fish swimming widely about and say, "Pick one". This always made me laugh. I would wave my hand recklessly and point quickly in every direction, and as excited as I could I would shout, "that one, and don't try to pass off an imposter for the one I chose either, I will know". He thought that everyone should eat fish at least twice a week. Once he found out of the *abuse* that I had suffered as a child, he did exactly what any loving understanding husband would do . . . he laughed at me and cooked more fish—more often. So, to say it was not a shocker that I forgot to feed his fish for 4 days after he passed is a huge understatement.

I had been doing so well with my grief, or so I thought. I measured good days by how many minutes lie between each outburst of tears. I had made it from 10 minutes to whopping 4-hour intervals at the point that I walked into the foyer that night and looked into the fish tank. I saw the two kissing grammies named **Denny & Debbie** (I hate fish remember. Therefore, you can't blame those names on me.) The kissing fishes were swimming nicely and sucking face like two healthy suck face fish should do. But there in the corner lying on his side, no longer looking black, but instead a dark gray, was Mr. Al G. Fish himself. He was not moving, he was not looking natural and giving me the usual, "I know you hate me so don't even try to hide it lady" look. I tapped on the glass (of course I did), and it suddenly occurred to me, that *just like Dennis he was dead*. Oh my God I can't begin to tell you where my mind went.

It started quietly with my announcement to my daughter that "Sarah, I think, oh no, Sarah, I think, Oh my God Sarah you are not going to believe this but I think, . . . no I am pretty sure that (tap, tap, tap) . . . OHHHHHHHH MY GOD (tears falling) I KILLED DENNIS' FISH!"

Ok, that really does not begin to cover the hysteria that ensued as I stepped through all the reasons that I was solely responsible for the end of ole' Al's life but there I was sobbing uncontrollably. My poor Sarah. She was 16 years old and quite ahead of her time, but she later said, "I had no idea how to console my Mom over a dead FISH, a dead Step-Dad yes, a FISH, noooooooooo idea!!" She did well. She said that Dennis was fishing in heaven and he just came back and "got" (i.e. caught) him. I cried harder and yelled, "Yes because he knew that I would KILL him if he didn't!"

We all know looking back it was never about the fish. It was one more little piece of Dennis gone. It was one more death, one more loss, just one more thing I couldn't save at a time where everything seemed unfair and everything made me cry. I don't know if Dennis got to fish up in heaven but I am certain of one thing . . . if he did, when he pulled Mr. Al G. Fish out of "big pond in the sky", he looked into his net and within twenty heaven seconds or less, all the angels heard Dennis say . . . "Hey you look just like my fi.s . . . . oh my . . . Debraaaaaaaaaaaaaaaa!"

NOW FOR THE REST OF THE STORY . . .

(I was raised on a lake—I can tell a fish story with the best of them)

As you just read I was not the "fan of fish" but because the tank, the fish, the entire idea of what Mr. Al G. Fish and the tank represented for Dennis, I had to keep it going. Besides, the guilt I was feeling over Mr. Al no longer being with us was just more than I could take. I did not know the first thing about caring for fish, cleaning a tank or anything of the sort. So, I did what any seemingly intelligent woman of today would do . . . I "googled" it.

I found a good man who lived nearby who knew more about fish and tanks than anyone should. He came to my house monthly, cleaned it, and tutored me on fish food, tank parts and all that was necessary to keep the one thing that Dennis had loved since he was a kid . . . *alive*.

To my surprise and joy this person also was what I learned to be somewhat of an "artist" and helped me create a new "world" for the fish in which to live. We upgraded to live plants, pretty colored rocks and what turned out to be something that turned Dennis' fish tank into a living memorial to him. He hand crafted a cross in a large rock, found a stone with a heart shaped hole already in it and built by hand a wooden cover for the tank that made it look like a treasure chest.

Once this was done, there was one more trip to the pet store made as we had to bring home the newest member of the our family . . . . Baby **Al**ley !! She is a 2 inch long, black, ugly, scaly, big lipped algae eating fish just like her Grand-pa-pa Al. I would like to say, "Long may she live", but you know . . . ?

OCTOBER 2011

(Facebook daily posts)

By The Grace Of God

10/04/2011:

Each day would end with dinner, Fox News, you & me alone talking about our day, the kids, decisions to be made, sharing funny stories and just relaxing with our best friend. It has been replaced with sorting through paperwork, making decisions that I would hope you would make or be proud of me for making, praying, reading and trying desperately to keep you alive in my memory, some smiles, more tears, emotional exhaustion and Sarah promising it will all be ok. May God keep you until I can once again hold you.

10/04/2011:

I went to work today. I wouldn't say I accomplished a lot of work but I did better than I thought I would. I called the roofing company that Dennis had scheduled and fired them only because after I explained that he had passed the man tried to tell me "but I have a signed contract" . . . that conversation ended with "you can't take dead people to court". I then called another who was recommended by our neighbor, he came out, I got a lower quote and when he said "you have a lot of hail damage who is your insurance company?" I called our insurance company (who had denied our claim once) and reminded them of why I have paid premiums for so long and that they "would" come back out and reassess the situation. Channeling my husband today I was.

10/04/2011:

Do your family a favor . . . make a will, get all paperwork in order, have insurance to pay off the mortgage, have life insurance, cover them in the event that God calls you home. It's the best thing you can do for your family.

10/05/2011:

Yesterday I drove to the insurance company. Just before I got there I saw a sign that said CHRISTIAN BOOKS . . . I whipped the car in the drive and ran in the store not knowing why I was there or what I was searching for. I think however, in my heart I knew I just needed an answer. I was the only person in the store besides the older lady behind the counter. I walked the entire store and looked but again I didn't really know what I was looking for. This lady said "can I help you" and before I could get the first word out the tears began to roll. I was so embarrassed and started to apologize and said "my husband died and I need to know he . . . is ok, can you help me." She came around the counter, walked me over to this chair to sit me down and then she got down on her knees, wrapped her arms around me and started to pray out loud. She told God I was too young to lose the one I loved but he must have been special if God needed him up in heaven and called him home. She prayed for my healing and to relieve the pain that I was feeling and to replace it with sweet memories of my husband and our time on earth. When she was done she went and picked up 4 books, handed them to me and said, "I lost my husband a year ago and I know what you are feeling, it's going to be ok". She went on to explain that she and her husband were 60 something and she felt even at their age they were "cheated" out of their time together so she could not imagine how I felt being this young and losing the one I loved. I bought the books, hugged her, thanked her and walked out. I now know that God made me see that sign, God had me pull in, HE put that sweet lady and I in that place at that time . . . and HE gave me more than one answer to my questions. I thought I would share this with you all. I hope you don't mind.

10/05/2011:

I am going to lobby congress, or whomever decides these things and I am going to have WIDOWED removed as the word used when you lose your spouse, and then it shall be replaced with a better word . . . LOVED !!!

10/05/2011:

I am pretty sure Dennis is up there right now talking to Steve Jobs about what he thought the IPAD could have done better! LOL. RIP Steve Jobs . . . you seriously changed our world!

10/05/2011:

If I may . . . "Don't let your hearts be troubled. Trust in God, and trust in me. There are many rooms in my Father's house; I would not tell you this if it were not true. I am going there to prepare a place for you. After I go and prepare a place for you, I will come back and take you to be with me so that you may be where I am." John 14:1-3"

10/05/2011:

I had a little talk with Dennis this morning. I don't know if he heard me because just like most men, he probably wasn't listening. I updated him on all the decisions being made, how I felt, and that yes I was a little "ticked" that he had to leave me this soon but I was sure God was all-knowing. I told him I wanted a sign that he could hear me or I was going to give away his dogs . . . It was then I stepped out of the car and nearly tripped . . . that made me laugh . . . I was like, "OK OK no need to get nasty about it."

10/05/2011:

The paper came today from the Social Security office said, "you are entitled to a ONE TIME death benefit" . . . and I thought . . . that's cool cause exactly how many times do you think he could pull that one off "

10/06/2011:

When they say "tomorrow is not promised" . . . they are not lying . . . turn to the one you love, hug them with all your might, tell them what they mean to you and how proud you are to call them friend, family, your love, your life. Tomorrow could be too late . . . truly. Dennis & I could fight like cats and dogs but we never left each other without an "I love you" even if it was through gritted teeth (lol). I am so thankful now that was the way we chose to love one another.

10/06/2011:

Ok if I am grossing anyone out with all this morbid death talk you can block me for a few months, I will understand. I just found the most beautiful urn that is made of maple, it has a trout jumping out from the water, ducks flying overhead, mountains in the background, two people in a canoe, it is so DENNIS and so perfect. It will be inscribed . . . LOVED DEEPLY—MISSED TRULY—REMEMBERED FOREVER, with his name and dates. It is very well done and tasteful. Had he been looking at it from a "different perspective" I am sure he would have approved!

10/06/2011:

I was behind him in the Taco Bell drive-thru in Jacksonville. We had just left each other and we were going to grab some food and head to our separate homes. He stopped his car in the drive-thru about 3 cars ahead of me, opened the door, got out and motioned for me to get out too. I opened my door stepped out of the car and he yelled for the first time ever, "I LOVE YOU!" I said later, "You know I love you too, but when we have to tell our grandkids you said it first at Taco Bell, I swear I am going to lie and pick a classier restaurant!" That was us!

10/06/2011:

Dear Dennis:

You thought you weren't loved, you thought no one wanted to be your friend, you thought that people didn't understand you but all awhile you were admired, respected, adored and looked up to. You were a man, you were not perfect, nobody here is, but you were very special and while you thought what you tried to give was not respected or accepted, it will be years from now when those you gave too will realize how precious your gift really was. Rest well my love.

10/06/2011:

I just want to say THANK YOU again to each of you on my list of friends. You have no idea how much your words, prayers, and kindness has lifted the kids and I. I know they call this a loss, but to me this is beyond loss. The ONLY way I can smile each day and move forward is truly to take the glass half empty/half full view. Meaning instead of "Dennis and I have been apart now 11 days" . . . I choose to think, "This is one day closer to the day we meet again." I am not in a hurry to leave earth. I have things left to do. I have children to watch graduate, I have grandbabies to rock to sleep, I have stories to tell and friends to lift up, but when my day comes . . . I will leave knowing I will be meeting GOD and seeing the love of my life again.

10/07/2011:

I don't know that I would say this morning was easy. I talked to God and told him about Dennis, and then realized he knew him better than I did. I talked to Dennis and asked him to guide me from up there. Dennis thought GPS was one of the greatest inventions so I am going to use the DBGPS (Dennis Bujanowski Guidance Proof System) when I don't know what to do or where to go I will count on Dennis to guide me. I am sure his personality was strong enough (ha) to make it through the clouds down to me!

10/08/2011:

Dear Dennis:

You would be so amazed at the generosity of your friend James and his family. He is a blessing and a true friend. He has been here for us and continues to be here for Timothy and I am so incredibly grateful for that. I cried for you this morning, I missed you so strongly but I also smiled over a couple of "that's so Dennis" moments.

10/08/2011:

I talked to the coroner yesterday. Not something that everyone can say they do on "any given day" hey? She is going to send me the autopsy report on Monday and then get on the phone and go over each part of it with me. She said the blessing is that he must have never stepped on the ladder, as there was no sign of him falling or injury in that way. Thank you Jesus as I was so scared that had happened to him and I am so thankful that now I know it didn't.

10/09/2011:

WOW today was very hard. We missed you so much today. Sundays were ours. You and I relaxing and preparing for the week to come. Kids are having hard moments, I am on edge and that doesn't help. Praying for you my love . . . if you can see us know we love you so very much.

10/09/2011:

They say grief can take on many faces . . . well today I am pissed and hurt. I am mad at God and mad at Dennis, and while neither one was to blame I am still mad. I want him back and I don't want to do this alone. Death sucks!

10/09/2011:

Dennis used to like to watch Joel Osteen (Ministry) on TV. I woke early and turned on the TV, saw it listed and watched. His message? If you have suffered a loss and there is no answer to WHY, store it in an "I don't understand file" and move forward. God has promised a new day, new beginnings, if we believe and trust in the Lord. I could continue asking why Dennis is gone, or I can move forward and trust in the Lord. Funny how things are put in front of you when you need them the most.

10/10/2011:

One small step for mankind, one large step for Debra . . . going to the school OPEN HOUSE tonight. I am going to try to see if there is anything I can volunteer to do that would make our schools better for the teachers and kids. God left me behind for a reason right? Just need to find where he can best use me.

10/10/2011:

Dear Dennis:

I went to Open House today at the school and ALL BUT 1 teacher said Sarah Jane DOES NOT TALK in class !!! OMGosh that made me smile, cough, choke, I mean smile with pride! I thought of you instantly and could hear you say, "REALLYYYYYY????" like you would always say. They say she's growing up. Keep watching babe, she is going to make you proud. Missing you down here.

10/10/2011:

So many memories . . . please people be grateful for what you have, love those around you and if you are going to leave a legacy, let it be a good one.

10/10/2011:

I came home tonight to a HUGE CARE PACKAGE from my son's employer. Household items, cleaning supplies, canned goods, paper products . . . the generosity and kindness of others is overwhelming sometimes. We are so very grateful

10/10/2011:

They say that most people can count their friends on ONE hand. I think that I would have to be part octopus or something because I have so many loving, caring, sincerely beautiful friends and your love, support and prayers are pulling us through. I know Dennis would be so very grateful to each of you!

10/10/2011:

Dear Dennis, my love:

I am doing it. I am going out into the world. I am pushing forward and onward and you better be watching me and hanging with me, after all there's probably no ESPN up there so it's not like you are busy or anything! I miss you!

10/11/2011:

Dear Dennis:

I don't think heaven is on EST so it may not be 730 a.m. where you are at, and for all I know you don't require sleep up there either, so since you LOVED mornings so much I am sure this is a huge bonus that you are enjoying. I am trying to picture you without coffee but just can't pull that one off quite yet. I love you sweetheart.

10/11/2011:

Dear Dennis:

Tim and I took the truck and went to Home Depot and purchased the rest of the materials needed to finish the job you had started that Sunday. You remember? You and I were there at 11:00 a.m. on that day. Less than 2 hours later you were gone. It still doesn't seem real at times. Remember how you used to always tell me that I was not the one to pay attention to "a deal" or just didn't "do the math" to know if I was being over charged? It is with that in mind and admiration for your never ending abilities to save us a dollar, that I share this with you. I was purchasing the primer needed and the clerk put 2-1 gal. cans in the cart. They were $15.00 plus each. As I walked away I saw a 2 gallon bucket of the SAME primer for $10.00 less. Replacing the two with the one, I looked straight up and said out loud, with a beaming smile, "Ha ! See Dennis I can do it too!"

10/12/2011:

Dear Dennis:

Well your urn came today. It's beautiful and if the circumstances were different I am sure you would love it (smile). I hope you are watching because not only is this your final resting place for your earthly body, but you also now have Sabbath, your favorite black lab buddy, in there with you to keep you company. I knew you would be okay with this as your answer to "how long is that dog going to adorn our dresser?" was always, "He goes when I go Debra." I love you so and my heart aches every day without you here.

10/12/2011:

My husband has been gone now what will soon to be 3 weeks. As many of you know, he was only 46 years old and so very loved. While I comfort in the fact that he is resting in the arms of Jesus and no longer subject to any earthly pains, worries or troubles . . . we miss him so much. I ask for your prayers for myself to be strong for my children, and to ease the pain that this loss has brought to those that loved him so.

10/13/2011:

Thank you Jesus for friends. They are the greatest gift a person can give themselves!

I love mine . . . hear me people . . . I LOVE YOU!

10/13/2011:

(To my daughter Sarah)

Sarah—you know he loved you more than anything in this world and only wanted what was best for you. He wanted you to succeed and be happy and he always loved how smart you were. It's ok to miss him and to cry, but in the end let's make him proud and show him that all of his effort, hard work and love paid off.

10/13/2011:

Dear Dennis:

Your work car is officially mine. I had a struggle with one insurance company today but I prevailed, (I just channeled you—ha). It was a long day, I missed you terribly and Sarah is missing you bad tonight. It hits each of us different at any given moment that you are not here. I was touched by a sweet note from your coworker today . . . my dear you were so loved and respected . . . I hope you knew.

10/13/2011:

I rearranged my stuff in the room so Dennis is on my nightstand. It makes me feel good to know he is nearby me when I wake and lay down at night. I start each day with a prayer for him and then one of thanks for all we have and for strength to get us through. One day at a time. Today his company is sending an advisor over to assist with misc. paperwork, so that is a blessing as I see it.

10/14/2011:

Dear Dennis:

These kids miss you so much. I know you didn't want to leave us anymore than we wanted you gone, but you were so much a part of each moment of our lives and our future, there is such an incredible void to fill in our hearts. Praying for you and loving you so.

10/14/2011:

Losing someone feels like your heart is ripped out, like you are walking in nearly dried cement, and every decision and thought is a major effort. It does get better day by day but in minuscule increments. I know it's hasn't been that long but the longest we were ever apart was 3 weeks and we swore we would never do that again. Now someone else has made that decision for us. Praying is all I can do.

10/15/2011:

Dear Dennis:

James came over today and he and Tim finished the work on the house. OMGosh you would be so grateful and proud. He had to think highly of you to do what he has done for us. I painted the windows on the garage, and around the front door and only had 2 meltdowns (as I call them) today. I find it nearly impossible to not think of you at any given moment. I pray for healing and your heart and soul. Loving you sweetheart always.

10/17/2011:

Sarah Jane just called me from the phone intercom while we try to figure out where our 700 handsets are currently hidden. Dennis used to do this all the time and when I would answer he would say in a very nasally/dorky voice, "Hellllloooooooooooo".

Sarah just did this JUST LIKE HIM . . . and said, "Did that make you smile? I am going to do that for you for the rest of your life!"

I said, "Thank you Dennis Jr.!" Isn't she the best?

10/17/2011:

Grateful for these things today: Dennis' closest co-worker came by to pick up his work items and while I was dreading just another piece of him to be taken away, it turned out to be a blessing as we shared a few of the things we loved about Dennis and laughed at some of his sillier moments.

I made it through work okay. I sold my first pair of earrings at the local salon. God is healing my heart a tiny piece at a time.

My husband was so loved and respected and God is showing me that more and more every day.

10/18/2011:

Dear Dennis:

I can only be strong for so long and it seems we are still in increments of "hours" not days. I miss you so much it just hurts and the tears seem to have a will of their own. I try to stay so busy that I just drop into bed exhausted so I have no time left to think but that doesn't seem to do the trick quite yet. Are you missing us up there because I feel like a part of me went with you and I haven't yet found how I am supposed to function without those parts. This will make you laugh Dennis, I bought "Auto Repair for Dummies". Remember how I used to say I refuse to buy those books because I found it wrong to think of myself as dumb ha. Please watch over me while I sleep and may God comfort me with dreams of you.

10/18/2011:

Dear Dennis:

You would be so proud. I didn't give up and I played it smart and GOD sent me a special man in a roofer who sincerely is honest and wanted to help me out. I got $3600.00 off the cost of replacing the roof on the house. As I shook the Insurance District Manager's hand he started with, "We were here before and there was no damage . . . and I understand you want this inspected again, but our adjusters are very thorough". I said, "What date were you here and what date did hail hit our town last?" They looked at each other dumbfounded. No answer given. I said, "That's ok, I know the answer to that and so do you, as you didn't drive across the state of South Carolina without knowing, so gentlemen let's get started and thank you for coming."

10/18/2011:

Dear Dennis:

I went to get the license plate last week when I bought your work car. The lady at the DMV laid out two plates for me to choose from as our state has two designs. One was all numbers and one started with letters. I looked down and the plate said, HNU-925. My mind immediately thought, "H-eaven N-eeded U . . . on 9/25". OMG . . . that was amazing. Since then (won't go into the huge story why) but I was asked to turn that plate back in due to some mistake they made BUT was given HNU-917 instead. 9/17 My Dad's birthday. I know heaven needed you both. Loving you . . . Debra

10/18/2012:

I would like to proclaim that TODAY WAS A GOOD DAY! Thank you Jesus and to all my friends for helping it to turn out this way.

10/19/2011:

While my heart is broken, every day I turn on the news and hear the MOST TRAGIC stories one can imagine. I think, "OMG I feel this bad and I know you are with GOD, those dear people lost everything and everyone, or their baby, or evil came into their lives while they weren't protected or aware." It's true no matter how bad you have it, you just have look around and you will find someone who has it worse.

10/19/2011:

Dear Dennis:

This week would have been OURS, this week we were on vacation, your aunt and uncle were coming to visit and we were going to cook together and laugh and get caught up because it's been too long. They are still coming and I am still going to make this a home of welcome, love and something you would be proud of . . . I know there will be tears, but we can also remember you for the wonderful, silly, funny and loving man you were. Missing you more than you know.

10/19/2011:

I want to be normal again, I want my heart to not hurt, I want the kids to be ok, and I want to go to bed and wake up and not feel this overwhelming sadness. I know everything takes time and while it feels like he has been gone forever I am struggling to believe it has actually been 24 days. What will today bring? A few more tears, a few smiles, lots of hard work, many prayers and hopefully God's healing for our family.

10/19/2011:

I am going to have a yard sale next weekend, so I started to sort through the closet and some of Dennis' dress pants. You should only know how many times I got onto this man about not emptying his pants pockets and having things go through the wash. Well, he is laughing at me now . . . I am up to $14.00, thank you baby!

10/21/2011:

Ok I know you all are probably thinking I have lost it but today Sarah and I went out and got "nail therapy" and had lunch and laughed. Sometimes the heartache is too dark and you have to run toward the light. We did this, we ran. While I was drying my nails under the lamp the young woman drying her pretty toes across from me started talking. She ended up saying "when my husband died a year and half ago." It is true God puts you where you need to be. Talking to her was comforting and brought me hope. God is good.

10/21/2011:

Today our mailbox was overflowing with cards of love, support, and words of how others thought of Dennis. It made me feel so good to hear how others loved him too and to know that my friends are still supporting us all these days later.

10/21/2011:

Dear Dennis:

Sarah is having a big miss you day. She is not alone. She is off today so we are going to go out and have a Mom & daughter day to see if we can get our minds off of things if only for a couple of hours. Watch over us baby as I know you will. I believe there is no measure of time in heaven so my love for you is eternal just as your new life with Jesus.

10/21/2011:

Dear Dennis:

Missing you this morning my friend. Wish we could have our coffee while we share the room with no words until the morning cobwebs clear out! While I believe you have answers now to questions that taunted you while here on earth, I am sure you know that how much I loved you then and love you now was never in question.

10/22/2011:

I see that my hair is graying so much and I don't want to color it. I see that I need to lose weight and I am going back to taking control of this. I see the ACTIVIA commercial and I have decided that I want to be the next Jamie Lee Curtis, she is so pretty, sexy and classy for her age, so I asked my friend to call me JLC all day! HA. A girl has got to dream right?

10/22/2011:

Today was special. Today I spent with a friend. We laughed, we shopped, we shared things about ourselves, we ate some awesome food (lol), we bought a few really cool things, and I got to relax, just get away for a while and not feel the weight of all that has happened on my shoulders. It was a great day and all the while I felt Dennis was with me. I am pretty fortunate to have such a strong, smart and handsome angel looking out for me and my kids.

10/22/2011:

Proud moment #12. I went to my stock brokers office, had our $$ in stocks changed over to me and signed up for a class next Wed. after work to learn about buying and selling stocks (just the basics). I thought . . . "He did it, why can't I?" He would love that I am doing this, I know.

10/22/2011:

Today I go out and do a little thrift shopping with my friend! Much needed adult, girl, get away time . . .

10/22/2011:

Sometimes you are in so much pain you feel that it's ONLY you that this has happened too, and then you realize that you are not in an exclusive club. You drown out the sound of your heart breaking and your tears falling, you look and listen and find that "No, it was just your turn." When I get overwhelmed I think about 9/11/2001 and how all those spouses, siblings, parents and children felt when they realized their loved ones were not coming home. It makes losing Dennis no less tragic but it puts my grief into perspective in some odd way

10/23/2011:

Dear Dennis:

Today they confirmed what we have always known about you . . . you had a BIG HEART! They call it "enlarged" and they called it "sudden death". It definitely was that, but no matter what they call it, you are with God in heaven and your soul is protected while your heart remains here with each of us. We love you.

10/23/2011:

Some things there are just no preparing for. I read the autopsy today through tears.

10/23/2011:

Dear Dennis:

I pray that this week brings peace to all of us that are missing you so very much. Moving forward is so very hard but you find that with God all things really are possible. I have made some very short term, small goals that I will remain focused on while I take care of our family in a manner that would make you proud.

10/23/2011:

Is there a law against teenagers? Dennis you suppose you could talk that one over with God please?

10/23/2011:

I choose to believe . . .

10/24/2011:

Today I did something for me. Dennis' first gift to me was a diamond heart pendant. The chain I broke years ago. Today I went and purchased a strong new chain from where D bought my diamond ring. The jeweler asked me to pick out a plain band. He then asked for Dennis' full initials (which were mine also) and our wedding date. He said, "I would like to give this to you as a remembrance of him, please come back Wednesday and pick it up". Can you believe that? People are just amazing sometimes.

10/25/2011:

Sarah is COOKING DINNER . . . (stop stompin' the clouds Dennis) . . . she is BLASTING a new version of SIMPLE MAN originally by Skynyrd and blowing out

Gma's hearing aid. I said, "Sarah turn that down you are blowing out Gma's hearing aid." Sarah yells . . . "I am just trying to re-live her youth for her". I was thinking . . . Ok, that song is from MY youth NOT hers.

10/25/2011:

If you knew my husband personally you would know there was no one else quite like him. To read all of my posts and how much we loved each other you would think that Mr. BUFFALO NEW YORK's final words to me would have been something to the effect of "you were the best thing that has ever happened to me, I love you, etc." but God had other plans that day and remember God DOES have a sense of humor. Dennis' last words to me literally were, "I ate 6 CHICKEN WINGS!" When I thought of all the trips to Buffalo, all the times we went to the Anchor Bar (Home of the Original Chicken Wing), all of those wings we ate, all of the sauces we made and tried . . . I thought it was downright appropriate that a man from Buffalo. NY would go out saying that to his wife. God love ya' honey, I will never eat a chicken wing again that I won't think of you.

10/25/2011:

Dear Dennis:

A class in setting up a wireless network might have been helpful before you moved on there sweet pea.

10/26/2011:

Dear Dennis:

10/1/2006-10/1/2011

Dennis you received in the mail today recognition honoring your 5 years as a Field Service Tech III/Imaging Engineer with your company. You missed it by 1 week but I choose to think you were on vacation. It made me cry (of course) but it sure made me proud as it did the day you looked at me 5 years ago and said, "WE did it!" upon hearing YOU were hired. You were so amazing, so smart, determined and never failed to see any accomplishment as just yours. It was always US, OURS, what we accomplished TOGETHER. I live by your example today and each day going forward. I pray for you every day and I will love you with all my heart until my journey ends with US together again in each other's arms. Loving you forever, Debra

10/27/2011:

Gosh not a good morning. Woke up with bad headache, and even worse ♥—ache. I don't know what is making me miss you so bad this morning but I haven't been able to sleep since around 4 a.m. I want you home with us and yet know that can't happen. So, I say my prayers, put on the coffee, will get some crochet done and try to make the best of what seems never ending sometimes.

10/27/2011:

Dear Dennis:

I missed you today. Some minutes are harder than others, but because I always feel you are with me it tends to be easier as days go by. I am getting ready for our yard sale this weekend. I won't give up anything that YOU wouldn't have but I must tell you the first person who offers me .50 for the fish tank . . . SOLD BUDDY!

10/27/2011:

So I was in Wal-Mart tonight (of course), and I was talking to myself about the color of yarn (of course), and this older woman started talking to me (of course) about crocheting. We talked. It went from crochet to family to she lived in Jacksonville, Florida (Orange Park) for 30 years and then moved up here. She was so sweet and I am going to find her the crochet pattern she wants to make headbands w/ flowers so she can make them and donate them to the American Cancer Society. She is going to send me her old crochet book that shows all the stitches. I love making friends.

10/28/2011:

Mom wants to go "shopping" (oh no) but she needs to get out and have a little fun too. I think getting out into the real world makes our days shorter and easier to deal with. Of course I can't spend myself broke on retail therapy . . . or can I?

10/28/2011:

Dear Dennis:

It still seems strange to wake and you are not here. I have to clear the sleep from my mind when I wonder where you are and then it hits me again. I can't help but wonder what you would be doing if it had been me that left that day. I want to ask "Why?" but I don't . . . I just stop and pray and trust that God will make that clear to me someday. I miss you so very much.

10/30/2011:

Dear Dennis:

We were supposed to grow old together. Remember when you ask me to marry you and I said yes very quickly and you laughed and wanted to know why I answered so quick? The answer was, because I could picture us growing old together and I never saw that with anyone else.

10/30/2011:

Dear Dennis:

I told Sarah driving down the road today, you know 30 years from now I am going to be like, "AND YOU KNOW WHAT THE 832nd REASON IS THAT I AM PISSED THAT HE DIED?" I just seem to blurt out a new reason every few hours. Poor Sarah she is just now looking at me like I have lost my mind.

10/31/2011:

Dear Dennis:

This holiday reminds me of you. This was your Mom's birthday. The first year that you worked as a Bio-Medical Technician you worked in the local trauma center in our town. You came home with this beautiful bronze pumpkin that held a candle. It was the first year you could afford to buy me something "just because". Each year I would get a pumpkin of some type, a pretty candy dish, something that celebrated Halloween. I have all of those items out now and each time I pass through that room I think of how proud and happy you were to give me that gift each year and how I grew to anticipate our little tradition. It is things like that that I will carry with me for the rest of my days as a part of the love we shared.

10/31/2011:

So many of you have reached out to me since I lost Dennis. And some of you have expressed that while you wanted to share something with me you were cautious, as you did not want to offend me or upset me during this sensitive time. My life has always been an OPEN BOOK—that's how I roll. lol. I love to share my home, my family, experiences, knowledge, talents, heart and prayers . . . but at the same time that I am giving I LOVE to receive in return. I love when YOU reach out to me with a kind word, an experience, how you have shared in my grief because you lost someone too, a scripture (from any religion), a poem (from any viewpoint), something that someone told you that helped you. You CAN'T offend me, it's nearly impossible because I have already called you friend, and that was not by chance. I am very selective who I call friend and if you are my friend I know that what you do is done in the name of love. So please do not hold back—I need you now more than ever. Love you all my friends.

SPEAK TO ME

I have never been "religious" as some people say, but I have always believed. I was not raised attending church. I always thought that GOD was a secret that others knew but I was not privy too for some reason. I used to be so turned off when I would hear on TV of the man who killed a family of five, went to prison and then "found God". Really? You found him did you? Where was he hiding I wanted to ask? Right there on C block was he now? Why didn't you find him before you picked up that knife or that gun? It all seemed like such an easy excuse or thing to say to make you less of the monster that you really were. I couldn't understand how you could just say you were "saved" and it was so. What I am telling you is . . . I didn't get it.

Dennis was raised Catholic but wasn't a practicing Catholic I guess is the best way to say it. He was just out of the Navy when we met. He was living the fast and hard life of a young man with no real direction or boundaries. He loved to party with his friends, stay up all night and did as he wished. I never thought that Dennis didn't believe, I just never believed that Dennis "had the time for God" at this point in his life as young people sometimes do. I, on the other hand was not raised "anything" other than with love. I gave my life to Christ in my twenties and was baptized. I did not belong to a church either at this point in time.

So there we were. We both gave our lives to Christ. We both believed but neither of us gave God the time and glory as we should have when here HE had given us life. As the years went on I would read the Bible and discuss passages with Dennis and we would pray together. I felt secure in God's love for me, for Dennis and for my children but I knew I was not where I should be in my faith.

How tender we are in our thoughts and our hearts when we are young. God made us this way you know. Innocent, naïve and actually fearless to take on the world and live without abandon. Eyes and hearts wide open. You only close your eyes tighter and secure the perimeters of your heart when something hurts, attacks or offends. You learn to build walls, shut down, and protect. You *learn* fear. But until you learn these things you are as new and open to every beautiful moment that life and love have to offer. This was us for the most part. We did this Dennis and I. We lived as if there were no tomorrow, without abandon, loving all the way, no fear, no walls, protected by God we prayed and motivated and strengthened by our love for each other.

I continued with my Bible study and struggled for understanding. As life began to play out I was beginning to think that maybe God didn't really hear me or love me as much as others. It didn't exactly seem he was blessing us when I miscarried our baby, when Dennis' Mom passed away suddenly on my Mom's birthday and Dennis' first day of his new job, when my children were living so far away in Buffalo due to a messed up divorce and custody battle. It didn't seem that I was "saved" from anything. It pretty much seemed to me that I was going to be given my share and then some.

I listened as others said, "God speaks to me". **Why wasn't God talking to me?** I don't understand and someone explain to me who the Holy Spirit is that "moves" through so many and "works" in so many but apparently not in me. Was I still not privy? All I can do is go forward I thought, do my best to be a good, caring, loving individual and maybe God will get back to me with all of my answers soon enough. Just hang in there Debra, I told myself, you couldn't possibly be so bad that God has forgotten you. Just keep reading his word.

As we all get older we think harder and longer on our own mortality. I think that is just the way life works. You are young, you think nothing can happen to you and you will live "forever". You marry and say "until death do us part". Those are "just words" that are written in every vow since the beginning of time, are they not? You never actually expect that death will come to make good on that statement. There will always be a tomorrow.

When the last tomorrow actually came, and death actually did "do us part" I had a choice to make. Do I start to build the wall now, do I no longer believe, do I hide behind the pain and the fear of my unknown future, do I become bitter and paralyzed so by grief that God would "do this to me" or do I forge ahead and leave the questions of "why" for a later meeting with our Lord?

What a choice hey? No matter which path I choose at this point, there is pain, there is fear, and there are so many tears that I can hardly carry the bucket I store them in. No matter which path I choose I walk it now *alone*, I do not have him standing by my side holding my hand. He always made everything ok. Dennis always made it all better. Now I walk without him. Now I am alone. Or so I thought.

All of those years ago we gave our lives to Christ remember? That very moment HE promised me *and* Dennis eternal life. He promised he would never leave me, he would always be by my side, and he would always guide me and always love me. HIS promise was "I will not forsake you". He is there as I choose between putting down the tools used for building those walls and try to be open to let love come to me again. He is there as I say I can't go on without him, I will never love like that again, I don't want to start over, I don't know how to do this alone, I don't want someone new, no one will ever want me like he did or understand me. He remained with me when I got mad at him and cried for hours screaming "WHY? WHY HIM? WHY NOW?"

When the tears dried and the pain eased I knew that HE had been there through it all. But more importantly I know he is still here now. I knew that this was his plan for me and while I don't know what this plan is, I know I must be a part of it, I must move forward, I must do for myself so God can do for me. "God helps those that help themselves" isn't that we have all been told? I must honor the memory of those days of loving the man that I don't want to live without but now I am given no other choice. "You never know how strong you are until given no other choice". Ever hear those words? It's the truest statement I know other than "God loves you".

I can't remember the first four days that Dennis was no longer on this earth because I was in my bed, covers over my head in a puddle of tears and a sea of disbelief. I wore his shirt and could still smell his cologne. I stared at his picture and his shoes still sitting by the bed. I held his wallet in my hands and kept his favorite hat that he was wearing when he took his last breath next to me on the bed. I cried, I cried, I slept only for moments at a time, I woke and I cried some more. It was during these four days that the Holy Spirit spoke to me and said "I am with you". I heard that between my sobs of grief. I heard that and not with my ears. "I am with you". I now know the meaning of those four small words. Pull back the covers, stand up and go forward. Dennis is ok, he is with Jesus and he will always love you and so does God. You can do this, I made you strong, and I made you a Mother because I knew you were this strong. I didn't take Dennis to punish you I called Dennis home because I needed him. I would never do to you what I didn't think you could not withstand. I know your strength, I know your heart and *I am the wall that protects it.* You don't need to start construction because you are a child of God, and I've got you and your heart in my hands. Please stand up and live. I never heard a sound and yet I knew I had heard it all.

So there it is . . . the Holy Spirit was speaking to *me*. Remember when he only spoke to others and I felt left out? Why did the Holy Spirit only start talking to me now? Because it was now that I called on God. God was just waiting on me. He was there all along just waiting for me to reach out in faith that he would bring me through this heart wrenching grief.

When I gave my life to Christ, his promise to me was that he would always be with me. He would always love me. He would never give me more than I could handle, and above all he would speak to me through my heart and he would be sure that I heard *and understood* each word.

No, it does not take death to find God; it does not take death or loss to hear the Holy Spirit. However, when you are facing death and loss and you cannot "go on" or "do it alone", when you cry out to God because it seems this is more than you can possibly withstand, when life cannot proceed for another second because your heart is so paralyzed with grief, so incredibly broken, be still . . . this is when the Holy Spirit speaks to you. This is when you hear but not with your ears, this is when your heart and soul do the listening for you. This really is when God comes near.

NOVEMBER 2011

(Facebook daily posts)

Thankful

November 1:

Dear Dennis:

Time will not stop because you are gone. It's already November and I don't know how we got this far. Missing you no longer describes what I feel each day. I so long to hug you as you leave for work and hear your voice on the phone when you call me during the day just to "check in" and say hello, cuddle up with you each night and talk about the day's events. No missing you just does not begin to cover it . . . love you best friend!

November 1:

Dear Dennis:

Do you see us struggle and hear our tears fall? I don't think you do because that would cause you pain and there is no pain in heaven. I do believe that your spirit and ours became intertwined here on earth, so when you left that day you took a little piece of us with you . . . and it was the piece that held all our love for you! Continue to rest baby . . . you worked hard here and you deserve some peace. God loves you and so do I . . . forever.

November 2:

20 minutes exercise this morning. I am on the "I want to look like Jamie Lee Curtis diet/plan!" So far I can see a small resemblance. Ha.

November 2:

Just when I think I am "OK" it hits me again. I am sure my husband was up there going, "Pull over Debra, your driving stinks anyway and crying only makes it worse!" (No really he would say that!)

November 3:

I am not sure who started the RIP thing but when I die I want everyone to post this . . . . NMHW Debra. (**N**o **M**ore **H**ouse**W**ork).

November 3:

I have had much reason to ponder death lately . . . so as I ponder "how will we know our loved ones when we get to heaven" some say we will be a BIG ball of energy. I say I have carried this BIG ARSE of mine around long enough and I want to go as a "little, petite, size 2" ball of energy and if no one recognizes me . . . well . . . then . . . that's a chance I am willing to take!

November 3:

Dear Dennis:

I told the kids that if they heard thunder that was you jumping up and down on the clouds to get a message through . . . well it's thundering. What's up babe???

November 4:

Dear Dennis:

I think this was a good day. I exercised even though I didn't want to, I didn't bust out crying today (did enough of that yesterday), I made chicken wings Dennis! I cut them up, got the oil just right, melted the butter into the sauce, it was so yummy. Our life is still spinning without you here but I am just staying as busy as I can so I don't have time to think too much. Just before bed is hard but I still tell you I love you just like I did when you were here. Loving you from here.

November 4:

My husband loved to drink a glass of wine every now and then. When he died he left me with a HUGE Wine collection. So tonight I am breaking open a bottle and price items for the yard sale. Come tomorrow I will either be really broke with no stuff or really well off with a hangover! I will update you then . . . lol.

November 5:

Dear Dennis:

We had a yard sale today. I was ok with selling the things of yours that I did and I knew you would have been ok with my decisions, but honey when I got to the boxes of ties and saw the one you wore the day we married I LOST IT. Thank God for Tracy because she knew just what to say and do to make it better. She suggested we keep them ALL and I make something with them. So, I will be coming up with a sewing project that will be made of ALL of your ties. I miss you so much Dennis I can't even begin to tell you. I pray that I don't have to tell you that you somehow just know.

November 6:

I have decided that I will keep Dennis as my profile picture in some manner for a year from the day he passed. It brings me comfort to sign in and see him, and it makes the icon on my phone a picture of him. From that year mark I will start again with whatever mood hits me, but I do this in honor of him, our family and our love. So hang with me guys.

November 6:

I am trying to figure out if I am feeling overwhelmed because I really have "so much more" to take care of with Dennis gone, OR if this is the same amount but I don't have him to share it with, bounce things off of, absorb some of the "overwhelm-ness" that I feel. I miss my baby and best friend.

November 7:

Dear Dennis:

I wake up and go to sleep missing you. Everything in between is just what I "need" to do to make it through another day

November 7:

While we all know that death is a part of life, there is just no step by step on how it goes. How to handle it (even though one day at a time is good advice) has a way of taking you over at any given moment and rendering you helpless. Today was not good. I felt like I had come so far and today I was hurled back to the moment I lost him. I yelled at God as I was very angry and I cried and screamed at my friends that I knew would understand. And tomorrow I will start again and pray it is a better day than today. I have a few things left to do and then it's me and my pillow. For those of you who I talked to today—I love you and thank you for holding on!

November 8:

I love you Dennis James Bujanowski !!!! I am going to channel your strength today and see if I can make this a GOOD day !!! Sending you x0x0x0x0x !!!!

November 9:

Dear Dennis:

I can't stop missing you, as it's just not in me to do that. I won't stop loving you because there is nothing in me that ever could. I will never forget you because you can't forget those that brought you pure joy, true love, warmth and comfort, safety and peace. I will never be without you . . . for I carry you within my heart and soul.

November 9:

My husband has been gone 45 days. My son is preparing to graduate high school and is trying to decide what career choice he wishes to make in the U.S. Army. My daughter is IN LOVE, and I can't seem to make time slow down for even a second. When I said be grateful for what you have and tell those that you love that you love them . . . I was not kidding. In a blink of an eye my friends . . .

November 9:

One of the dearest friends in my life told me the other day it was OK to yell at God, that he would understand if I was angry and mad and didn't want to talk to him. I did just that . . . but I ask my friend to go to him in prayer FOR ME while I was getting over the latest wave of pain that rushed in that I was so nicely blaming HIM for. "Dear God, Debra is a just a little ticked at you right now . . . so I am going to do the talking for her . . . so here we go . . . tell Dennis . . . ." NOW THAT'S A FRIEND.

November 10:

Went and got my nails done yesterday. I used to do my own to save, but you know what? Now I have less than when I did my own and I am paying to have them done. This is going to be my ME expense every month. Why? Because I can, I want to and it makes me feel better. Besides that a girl just can't go around with man hands . . . one must remain pretty! lol

November 10:

For you Dennis . . .

We said we would grow old together, but that was not meant to be

We said we would last a lifetime, for all of eternity

You stood by my side that day in May what seemed just moments ago

I walked by yours each day after until God called you and said, "It's time my child to go."

I wish so much to touch your face, kiss your lips and tell you I will be ok

I await our reunion as I know you do, but for now I must delay

I have so much left to do and see, sharing all you will not miss a minute

I have a broken heart yes truly I do, but forever I carry you in it

So rest in peace sweetheart, your legacy of love through us is forever shown

I know it is God's will that we hold each other again someday, in a place we will both call home

November 11:

Dear Dennis:

Remember when I said "if you are ok, just give me a sign, make the cat talk, let Mocha (chocolate lab) get up and do a little dance, something, anything?" LOL. Ok, so you reach out to TWO of my friends that you did not know either for very long. You appear to one in a dream that I was in as well (same dream repeated 3 times and the 3rd time you were there speaking to me) and told me that it was ok for me to be happy ("but not too happy ok"—ha). The other person received what she described as strong suggestions to "tell her I love her, tell her, tell her". So, while I believe in very specific things regarding communication with the dead, I want to know why you are not making our cat talk or our dog dance???? COME ON DENNIS . . . don't let me down here honey . . . I know you can do this.

November 11:

Dear Dennis:

As I look at my profile picture of you as a little sweet pea, I think . . . My gosh we would have made some pretty babies!

November 11:

Dear Dennis:

Tim just left for a weekend at a GA Military College. I hope you are watching as he is growing into a man and I don't want you to miss a minute of this!

November 11:

Now this is a legacy. Tim said last night . . ." I hope I can be like Dennis when I grow up. Successful and smart and if I fall in love with a woman who already has children like he did you, I will take care of them like he did us, I wouldn't mind that at all". That about broke my heart and made me burst with pride at the same time!

November 11:

Dear Dennis:

I am making my first trip without you today. I am taking your black truck, your gps, your radar detector, your Mother-in-law, and Step-daughter and heading to Georgia where Tim is attending his military weekend. I know you will be riding with us and "spouting words" the entire way about my driving! (No road rage in heaven now sweetie!) Love you!

November 14:

They just don't make friends like the ones that Dennis and I call friends. I am still getting donations to Dennis' memorial fund. He would be so touched to know as this will help Timothy out with his plans for college. I could not be more grateful. Thank you all.

November 14:

Dear Dennis:

Whatcha doing up there? I know you are staying busy helping, or learning something that fascinates you that you did not know here on earth. I am missing you (of course) that is what I do every minute of every day. I try not to look too far ahead because thinking of being without you for months or years is more than I can stand to think of right now. I love you babe . . . I know you are here in spirit.

November 14:

If there ever comes a day when we can't be together, keep me in your heart, I'll stay there forever. (Winnie-the-pooh).

November 14:

Sarah Jane . . . while I appreciate you cooking dinner, I just want to pass on something that my Ma passed on to me from her Ma . . . you can't really call it cooking IF YOU DON'T TURN ON THE OVEN!

November 15:

I walked into the bedroom last night, sat down to crochet and this freezing cold air hit me. The fan was not on. The window was closed. I said, "Ok if that is you, remember that I need the cat to talk or the dog to dance to believe . . . you making it cold will only make me turn the heat up and that will cost more on the electric bill so I KNOW you wouldn't choose that to give me a sign, Mr. WERE YOU BORN IN A BARN?" LOL

November 15:

Up since 4 a.m. thinking of you. Getting crochet orders done and missing you over a cup of coffee!

November 15:

Timothy is going to MEPS (Military Entrance Processing Station) today and tomorrow. While there he will get his MOS (Military Occupational Specialty) for the U.S. Army Reserves. His MOM (Master of Much) will be worried as us Mom's do but I know he will be fine. Keep him in your prayers today and tomorrow for strength to get through the very beginning of what will be his career in defending our country! Dennis and I are so proud of you Tim and love you very much!

November 15:

Dear Dennis:

I can see you fishing on the banks of heaven, where all fish take the bait, they are all big and when you tell a "fish story" you don't get in trouble by the BIG GUY because he invented fishing so he gets it !!! I know I am sad you are not here, but they must be thrilled that you are there. Lucky spirits! Love you forever.

November 15:

This is not me feeling sorry for myself, but every year on my birthday my husband bought and cooked me crab legs. One year he and our friend coordinated a party and in the confusion they forgot the cake. So, he got a big platter, put a huge candle that we had around the house in the middle and arranged my crab legs around it. He came down the stairs singing HB, and was very proud of his "CRABCAKE" and the big SAVING of the evening. We did not have a perfect life but together we were a perfect fit and he made so many of my days so special. I am still a little pissed that he gets to remain 46 while I keep aging but I will be sure to take that up with him when I get there! Until then . . . forever loving you Dennis!

November 15:

Ok just one more Dennis story for the day (I hope you aren't sick of these) . . . when the kids started school this year, HE went online and found the school calendar and he marked his phone calendar (not for my birthday .noooooo . . . lol) for 11/16 "Report Cards Due—Ground Kids". He only added that last part to get to Sarah as she was sitting there when he did it. Well Dennis GUESS WHAT???? No one is GROUNDED and Sarah got a B in Science!

November 16: (My birthday)

It's my party and I'll cry if I want too! ha. OK, I am trying for NO TEARS today. Sarah is home sick, Tim is coming home from MEPS. It is raining and storming like crazy outside. I miss you Dennis but no more than any other minute since you left us. I know that it's time for new traditions, but today I think I will celebrate quietly in my PJs and remember some of the good times we had. Besides that . . . my brother called me at 7 a.m. to tell me he is still OLDER than me, so that did my heart good!

November 16:

Hello my people . . . I have had some of the BEST phone calls this morning from those that I love oh so much. I was going to click LIKE on each birthday message but I am old now and I can't click fast enough to keep up. Just so you know that I love each of you dearly and I appreciate all that you are doing to make my day "ok" and special. I have decided to TAKE MYSELF out to dinner to Outback tonight. I am sure they have crab legs. You hear me Dennis . . . you can come too baby!

November 16:

Dennis my love . . . Today was GREAT. No really it was. Of course I missed you, that is a given. We laughed at some great "Dennis moments" at dinner, but today I had so many of my friends and family pulling me through. The love, the calls, the messages on Facebook, the mail, the email, the visits in person, it was all good for my heart and soul. I am so blessed. Tim and I clinked those glasses tonight with a "Happy Birthday Mom" and a "Congratulations Tim" (He signed the papers today and is now in the U.S. Army Reserves). I knew you were seeing it all, and that you were there. Did you see they DIDN'T HAVE CRAB LEGS so just for YOU I had grilled lobster tail (oh my that was yummy). I go to bed tonight knowing that you are in a much better place than you ever were here, and knowing that while I must stay here for now I have so much support and love to lift me up until we meet again. Loving you always.

November 18:

I speak to God each morning. I thank him for this day and those that came before. I ask him to protect my children, keep my Mother strong, and use me in the best possible meaningful way he can to touch another's life, to make me a better Mom and friend. I ask him to deliver messages to Dennis every day to tell him how much I love and miss him. I pray for those defending our country and those making our choices for us and any special request that comes from another in need. Then I simply tell him that "whatever" comes today I will find "one good thing" about it and from it no matter how bad some things seem to be. I ask him to take over those things that I just can't do alone or for myself. (That's usually when he sends me one of you.) I believe and I hope you have something that gives you strength each day and carries you through. God Bless and have a great weekend.

November 19:

Dear Dennis:

Good Morning my love, I woke up missing you. Some days it seems so unreal still that you are gone. Some days I know it's true, I feel strong and I prevail, but others it can be like the life is sucked out of me and just getting out of bed is a chore. When those days hit, I say a prayer and send you a message before my feet hit the ground. I tell myself "get up long enough to get a cup of coffee" and from there I force myself on. Loving you from here.

November 19:

I just did one of the hardest thing a widow can do . . . I cleaned out "his" side of the closet. I saved those things that I can wear like his old big t-shirts that remind me of him and bring me comfort. I packed bag after bag for the Salvation Army. I sorted the t-shirts that are unique that will be used for a 't-shirt quilt' and then I sorted items to be given to Tim and then I looked over the area and knew once again my life had forever been changed.

November 19:

Can I tell you beautiful people who I love so much something? I appreciate so much all of the compliments and the word "amazing" being used to describe me but I swear to you that if any one of you, GOD FORBID were thrown into this horrid situation you would pull your strength from deep down inside and move forward with all that you had in you too. I am not any more special than anyone else. I just tend to wear my heart on my sleeve and feel that my life really is an open book. It's not really mine, it's God's and he is just letting me use it until he calls me home. So until then I will try to make the best of what I have been given. What I feel I feel strongly, that has always been me. I love intensely, I anger easily, I talk loudly, I laugh heartily, I cry deeply. I am nothing if not dramatic but I know no other way. You have NO idea how each one of you has helped me through this horrible time. You have given me a reason to smile, to get up, and you have let me grieve and mourn openly which has helped to heal my broken heart so much. Thank you for letting me share my life with you each and every day.

November 20:

Ok this is what made me cry this morning. Try to understand this thought (OMG I am a whack job sometimes). I am 47. Up to now Dennis is the longest I have ever been with someone. He is the love of my life. I was simply thinking, "ok, I could meet someone at 50, marry again and live together until we fall off donkeys going down the Grand Canyon on that trip we always wanted to take at the ripe age of 85" and then HE would be with me LONGER than Dennis. Yep that was it. That is what made me cry. Like somehow that negated my love for Dennis (which I know it never will) but Jesus Lord I cannot believe the thoughts that pop into my head and what makes tears fall from my eye balls! LOL

November 21:

Did you know that even if the titles to the cars are in both of our names, and whether it says Dennis AND Debra, or Dennis OR Debra it does not matter. I have to pay the courts a fee, have written appraisals from the dealership (which I just went and got), copy of death certificate and a check for $35.00 so the Judge can handle as a "small estate claim." I can then get DMV to change the titles to just my name in order to be able to sell, trade in, etc. Oh My Gosh the paperwork of the one left behind is never ending. It's crazy. I am assuming they do this to keep us so busy that we don't have time to think about our loss.

November 21:

Here we go again. Remember the roof and the fight with the insurance company? Now it is the plumbing that is backed up because the folks that installed a new heating and air vent ran it into the pipe and bowed the pipe and sent it angled in a direction that won't allow the water to flow. My garage is covered in water, the insulation on the vent work is filled with water. It's a mess. So, I had the plumber write the estimate stating what caused the issue and I called the Heating & Air company, asked for the Owner and very nicely, professionally, and bluntly stated that I wanted them out here today, I expected reimbursement and new insulation work done. We shall see. I will let you know how this one turns out. I see a new chapter to my book called, "When your heart is not the only thing that breaks".

November 22:

Trying to get through the next few days. This is not going to be easy. I am going ahead with making the full dinner for my family as Tim may be gone in the military next year, and we are still fortunate to have Mom with us this year, and who knows what life may bring me and Sarah in the year to come. With that said, while this breaks my heart to not have Dennis with me, I remain thankful for what I do have. May each of you have a blessed holiday with those you love!

November 22:

Dear Dennis:

The thought of making this dinner without you is killing me. The dishes that we have come to make "traditionally" and the day we spend together watching the parades and football. It will never be the same. I give thanks this year that you and I had so many years of love, friendship, sharing and joy. It's all I can do to get me through the first one without you. Please know sweetheart that from this holiday season and for each one moving forward I will always be thinking of you, carrying you in my heart and sending you my love.

November 23:

I talked to God this morning and told him as we were about to celebrate one of those "earthly" holidays I knew that my heart would feel Dennis' loss just that much more.

So, I asked him (as I do each day) to send Dennis a message that we love him, we miss him and each day we do all we can do to make him proud and keep his memory alive. Since I don't know if Dennis hears me, but I do know God does, I am letting him be the messenger.

November 24:

Cherry pie in the oven, Dennis' favorite. I made this one just for him. For the rest of the meal we shall have a traditional Turkey and fixings. I was up and dressed by 630 a.m. and ready to start the day. SJ's boyfriend is joining us today for dinner and once din din is over I shall spend the rest of the day crafting to get ready for shows. I hope each of you has a blessed day with your families. Don't eat too much—well go ahead, that's what the floor is for later. Stretch out and take in some Detroit Lions football!

November 24:

I thought I could make it through the blessing but that was not meant to be. Thank you Tim for taking the reins. Dennis we miss you so much today, this is way harder than I thought it would be. Other than that dinner was yum yum yummy.

November 26:

Dear Dennis:

I almost think I could live with the one big heart break moment if I didn't have to miss you every day after and feel the pain each time you come to my mind which is so very often. Our memories of you make us laugh often but sometimes the waves of you not being here just kill me. Ask God if you can have a weekend pass please. Loving you.

November 27:

Tonight Sarah and I cooked. I opened one can of ravioli and she opened 2. It was quite a gourmet feast!

November 30:

Dear Dennis:

I sure wish if you had to leave us you could have done so say in March so I had time to prepare my heart for the Christmas season. Jesus this is hard. You loved Christmas, this is when you became a kid again, you did all the selecting of gifts and everyone always LOVED what you decided on. You wanted all decorations up and everything to sparkle, glitter and shine. I can't bring myself to do this now. The kids and I have talked and decided on no tree just this year. It's just too hard right now. We miss you too much.

LACK OF PLANNING
ON YOUR PART

I have spent many years in management throughout my working career. Due to the nature of the job, my favorite saying became, "lack of planning on your part does not constitute an emergency on mine". I have thought of that saying so many times over the years. As my kids wake up in the morning and say things like, "Mom, oh my gosh I have to leave in 10 minutes for school and I can't find . . . (fill in the blank)" or it's 8:30 p.m. at night and a child proclaims . . . "Mom, I have a science fair project due tomorrow can you help me?" Any good mother naturally replies with "Why of course honey because every Mom worth her weight in newspaper, flour, dish soap and glue knows how to construct a volcano and make it erupt within 24 hours, not a problem sweet pea, let's get started!"

At my house if you apply that favorite saying, but somewhat modify it to my husband (who I loved heart and soul), it would sound more like this . . ." *lack of putting your things where they belong when you are done with them so you know where they are the next time you need them instead of just mindlessly laying them down so you can't find them later and making the entire household go into panic mode when you realize that you can't find them does not constitute a small crisis in my world because you are having a large crisis in yours".* (Whew !)

At least 2-3 times a month, I stood proudly on my soapbox and exclaim these words to the world, e.g. "the dogs" because by this time we had gotten to this point they were the only ones left listening as everyone with two legs was out looking for the "missing artifact."

Let me give you a prime example. Dennis (i.e. husband whereby my sun rose and set) and our son Timothy (pride and joy) had a "guy day". Timothy's grades have been much improved and his attendance at school was excellent, so it was decided that Dennis would take a vacation day and Tim would play "hooky" and they would go "just be guys". They had lunch, went to the gun range and let their testosterone run rampant as pretending they were "Dirty Harry" and shot at targets. Once targets were destroyed they left the state, headed into Georgia where they attended the drag races, i.e. John Force type stuff . . . like Nascar but no left turns, much louder and ends way quicker. They came home all spun up with tales of funny moments and memories to last a lifetime.

All was well in our world. Sarah and I enjoyed dinner out, a trip to Wal-Mart (where we buy those things that we wouldn't have had the guys been with us . . . shhhhh girl secret) and just hanging out together. It had been a long week, and as the day wound down, I had a plan. It involved a hot shower, my pretty new pjs, a tall glass of Publix ice tea (nothing better), my bed with its freshly cleaned sheets, and my Kindle (electronic reading device). I was going to finish that book that I have been reading one chapter at a time for weeks.

I was almost there. I settled into the cozy bed, got those pillows just right so I was propped up into the perfect position to read, had my buddy Molson (my loyal faithful black lab who follows me everywhere) on the floor at my side, my tea on the nightstand, my Kindle fired up. Yes, this was the life, this was what I had been waiting for all week, this was "Debra time in her sanctuary", this was relaxation at its best, this was . . .

. . . The moment Dennis busted through the door and exclaimed . . . ***"Holy Crap Debra, Get up and help me, I lost my frickin' wallet!"***

Just to add a little to this drama let me mention now . . . Dennis was leaving on a business trip in two days and clearly needed his driver's license and credit cards! Shoot me now . . . please . . .)

Let me interrupt my own story for a moment. I should have seen it coming. Which makes me think of the last episode of the Sopranos? Do you remember how it was all based on the premise of whether they were shot or not at the end? Do you remember how Tony and Bobby had a conversation of how when you were shot you "wouldn't see it coming"? Well, I should have seen this coming. I should have known that my "BLISS" was about to be "SHATTERED".

Are you like me? Do you know your family members by the sound of their footsteps and the way they walk? We have hard wood floors in our hallway that lead to the bedrooms. I can even tell you if it is my son, my daughter, my husband or which dog is walking in the hall by their cadence, the heaviness of the step and the dogs by the click of their nails on the floor. So as I read the first paragraph of my book, in the background I hear a heavy, steady, "man on a mission" type footstep getting louder and closer. I should have known. Yes this is Dennis and no he is not going to bust through the door shouting, "Dear God Debra you are the best thing that ever happened to me and I just couldn't sit out there watching ESPN a second longer without coming in here and confessing my love and affection for you!" No, I should have seen it coming.

So, now it's out there . . . the "missing artifact" has been identified . . . it is a wallet. One wallet that contains four credit cards, a large sum of cash and a driver's license with our home address. Our home address provided so someone can conveniently come directly here, break in and kill us in our sleep. Too bad he didn't tape the wallet to the GPS and lose that as a "package" so the killer could have typed "HOME" and had an easier time finding us in the dead of night.

You must now go through the "process". Ahhh yes the process . . . answer those 8000 questions that are meant to create the "process of elimination" and lead you directly to your lost article. Now I want you to clearly understand it is only because of Dennis' lack of . . ." on his part, that he felt "constituted an emergency" on my part, that got me sucked in to this drama and now I have identified my role as "Lead Detective" the person who is going to take charge, stay calm, rally the troops, asks the appropriate questions, and solve the crime. I will save the day! (Trumpets sounding) RED TEAM GO.

Debra initiates the ACTION PLAN, however very soon into it realizes that Dennis has now raised his blood pressure by say ohhhh 100 points. He is clearly in panic mode, he is angry at himself but since it is not in the male DNA to admit that . . . he will project his anger at me for being ridiculous enough to ask such unnecessary questions "at a time like this."

Debra: Where did you go today?

Dennis:—You know where we went, the gun range, the race track . . .

Debra: Did you use it there?

Dennis:—Well yes, that's pretty much how I paid to get in . . .

Debra: Where did you last see it?

Dennis:—In my back pocket DEBRA, where most people keep their wallets!

Debra: Did you look in the car?

Dennis:—Yes we looked all over the car

Debra: Did you look around the car?

Dennis:—Why would we do that?

Debra: Did you get a flashlight and look under the seats of the car?

Dennis:—Yes, Debra I said we looked in the car (eyes rolling)

Debra: Did you change your clothes when you came home or is that what you were wearing?

Dennis:—Is that really relevant Debra?

Debra: Did you go into the bathroom? Did you look in there?

Dennis:—Yes and I am sure I dropped it down the toilet (Hey now . . . there is no reason to get snarky)

Debra: Did you lift the cushions on the couch?

Dennis:—Do you not see them laying all over the living room?

Debra: Do you want me to call the credit card companies and report your cards lost?

Dennis:—Noooooooooooooooooo Debra (He YELLS as if I am the enemy) . . . here it comes . . . my favorite part . . . the "man" portion of my story . . . "Because I don't know I have "ACTUALLY LOST" it yet!

(Breathe Debra . . . you love him heart and soul, heart and soul . . . through better or worse . . . breatheeee . . . .)

"OHMYGOD . . . Ok, well then D-E-N-N-I-S when you "actually" (vision me doing the two handed—two finger—air quotation marks) figure out if you "actually" (again with the fingers) lost something could you possibly come back in and tear me away from our bed, my delicious glass of tea and the book I have been dying to finish now for weeks. Could you sweet cheeks? Yes could you come then and get me honey, sweetheart, love of my life? I will just be in the bedroom, that's right the one down the hall, yes sweetie that one, yes darlin' our "love nest" as you call it, where I was when you busted through the door exclaiming you had (voice jumps 12 octaves and BIG air quotation marks please . . .) LOST YOUR FRICKIN' WALLET"

Thirty minutes later, all family members engaged in the search, cushions ripped off of every couch, the car torn apart, the garbage has been gone through (not sure the logic on that one), every room searched high and low in true FBI fashion, by now the dogs have been clothed in bright orange doggy search and rescue vests, their noses to the ground in pure lab tracking fashion . . . . no wallet!!!

Dennis is defeated . . . he walks over and sits on the couch. He shakes his head. The actual thought that he has lost his wallet and all of its contents and what that indicates in terms of identity theft, security, financial loss and not to mention how this is going to affect his business trip is starting to really sink in. He slouches down on the couch, throws his hand to his forehead as if resigning to what is truly happening here. I hear a few whispers of "oh my God this is not good" . . . and it is at that very moment . . . he looks down . . . he stares hard . . . he drops his hand from his forehead . . . he starts to sit up slowly . . . as just in front of him under the edge of the coffee table . . . two inches from the end of his shoe where he was sitting the entire time before he took that long hard walk down the hall . . . was what? Yes, the "no longer missing artifact" . . . the WALLET!

Now, I, Detective Blood, wanted to ask how it got from the back pocket that he never took it out of and made it under the coffee table, but why waste any more time on those "non-relevant" questions "at a time like this". And I just want to make it clear that it had NOTHING to do with him removing his wallet from his back pocket, to take out his credit card, to do some internet shopping, from the laptop, from the couch, after dinner, while I was clearly unaware of the impending catastrophe headed straight towards my family. No it was not that so let's not even go there . . . (wink wink) The point is . . .

Drama over, crisis averted, flashlights back on the chargers, Sarah get out of the garbage, Tim kennel the search dogs, Debra put the cushions back on the couch . . . let's all resume life as we know it as we have just been spared by the grace of God of all things Lost and Found.

RED TEAM STAND DOWN . . . . Abort . . . Abort . . . Mission accomplished . . . . until next time . . . when the pounding of those footsteps down the hall will end with the door flying open and my charming, wonderful, loving husband proclaiming . . .

. . . " Holy Crap Debra, Get up and help me, I lost my frickin' CAR KEYS!!!!!!!!"

DECEMBER 2011

(Facebook daily posts)

Cold Winters Night

DECEMBER 2:

This morning Christmas music made me cry. Sarah said something that should not have made me cry and that made me cry. Missing you makes me cry, my stupid migraine made me cry. I think I have swollen eyeballs now. Dennis if you can hear me when I speak or even when I cry please know these tears are because no day is the same without you in it. I continue to pray, I continue to move forward step by step . . . one day closer to you!

DECEMBER 3:

Setting up our table last night at crafts fair a woman somewhat older than me strikes up a conversation. After a few moments she says, "I am sorry, I am so very sad. My husband has dementia and sometimes he knows me and sometimes he talks to me about me because he doesn't know who I am." I thought, God, here I am sad because my husband is no longer with us here on earth. How awful it must be for him to be here and "no longer be with us". I told her about Dennis, we both were clearly wearing our emotions on our sleeves at that moment, I hugged her and told her . . . "Tomorrow you and I can cry together while we sell our pretty stuff and people wonder why we are so weird!" Today she walked in, hugged me and smiled and just said only, "THANK YOU."

DECEMBER 10:

I asked Dennis this morning if he was feeling a little "dusty". I dusted his table off and his urn and all of his things that I have surrounding him. I told him I was sure that he appreciated the fact that I had moved the small speakers over to either side of his urn where I could blast some Rolling Stones for him every now and then. I know he is loving this.

DECEMBER 13:

I just received a call from Dennis' closest co-worker. He said he knew this time of year was hard and wanted to make sure that we were ok and to see if we needed anything. He said he misses Dennis every day and still cannot believe he is gone. After we talked he said, "Well Debra I called to see if I could cheer you up, but you have instead cheered me up with your attitude." I hope my husband knows how sweet his friends were and how much they miss him.

DECEMBER 13:

It's funny how long it takes business's to catch up with things. I advised CVS upon Dennis' death to close his account/profile so they would not be refilling any meds automatically. Today I get a letter from the pharmacy telling me that they can't fill his meds because his Doctor wouldn't authorize a refill !!! Really? Really? OMG. I can't imagine why not! LOL

DECEMBER 14:

Some days no matter how hard you try to be upbeat and cheerful, the loss is just too overwhelming. Today is one of those days. He should be here and he's not, and I am pissed and hurt and I want my best friend back. There . . . . now that I got that out . . . I shall go find something to laugh about . . . (The Big Bang Theory !!!)

DECEMBER 15:

Sarah and I were laughing at "Dennis moments". We were remembering the time we watched this "chick flick" all the way through, we get to the end of the movie where the guy and the girl finally get back together after the always dramatic breakup. In the last scene the man was at the beach playing catch with his dog . . . when the chick walks up he throws the ball, the dog runs off to catch it and the movie ends with the girl and the guy in the big hug/kiss final scene. Sarah and I were sighing at the love of it all when we hear Dennis say with the most sincerely distressed concerned voice . . . "But where did the dog go?" (Such a man moment!)

DECEMBER 16:

Since you left I have had to learn about stocks, annuities, probate, plumbing, roofing, insurance terms, and fish tank care. I thought I was a smart cookie when you were here (ha) but now I feel I know quite a bit more. I would trade it all for another moment with you but I know that "learning and knowledge" was what you loved the most, and so I shall continue to grow and make you as proud as I can. Miss you honey!

DECEMBER 16:

You do realize that the ONLY way you are GOING TO MAKE IT HAPPEN, is to think about it, talk about it, and then GET UP AND DO IT! You have more power to change things than you know. I am trying to improve myself while mending a broken heart. It is my hope that once I am done with my PIP (personal improvement plan) I will get to the last step and realize that while I was busy exercising, learning about stock trading, making new items to sell, growing spiritually . . . I will find that God was using that same time to heal my heart and I really will be ALL new again, and better for the good and bad that brought me to that point.

DECEMBER 16:

I used to tease Dennis and say, "I swear if you die on me I will take all of your life insurance and use it to rescue dogs!" HA! and along comes BUSSTOP (Stray pup we took in) . . . "See Dennis, I am a woman of my word !!!"

DECEMBER 18:

Really Dennis? I can get a new roof paid for, take over your stocks, buy your car, but let me try to download one little computer app and it kicks my butt every time. Could you just come down here for a minute please?

DECEMBER 20:

Dear Dennis:

Please don't be upset with me but I want to marry Elliott Stabler from Law & Order in either this life or the next. While I realize HE is not really real, I will settle for make believe just this once. He is just too cute! You understand right? Of course you do, it's that same thing you thought about Sandra Bullock!

DECEMBER 25:

Today I take comfort in knowing you are at peace, there is only joy and happiness in your life now. We remember you today with some tears as our hearts hurt but mostly smiles of all the funny moments you gave us. Until I hold you again please stay beside me and watch over Tim and Sarah. You would make the perfect guardian angel. Merry Christmas Dennis and please tell Jesus happy birthday for us. Always Debra

DECEMBER 29:

I just read, "God never tells us to do anything without giving us the ability to do it". Really? That's what God was thinking when he said, "Go forth Debra and remodel that bathroom !!!!????"

TWAS' THE MORNING OF CHRISTMAS

Twas' the morning of Christmas and all through the house

Not a Bujanowski was stirring, only the SPOUSE.

The stockings were hung on the doorway with nails

In hopes that Miss Debra hit all Walgreen Christmas sales

The children shuffled off to Buffalo for Christmas with Dad

Where visions of LAKE EFFECT SNOW were sure to be had

Ma Blood in her slippers, and I in my jammies

Had woken to Christmas howls of Mocha & Shami's

From down the hallway arose such a clatter

Dogs are barking in a furry," what the heck is the matter?"

Away to the kitchen I flew like a flash

**Forget the dogs, breakfast must be served,
biscuits, eggs and corn beef hash**

Catching my reflection in the toaster I see my beautiful hair

I am certain, oh so certain to cause the household quite a scare

And what to my wondering eyes should appear

But a big burly hunk of a man who I love oh so dear

With a request for coffee, and a remote in hand

I knew in a moment it must be MY MAN

Growing excitement from outside the barks came and came

He whistled, and shouted and called them by name

Now Molson, now Mallard, Shami and Mocha the Mrs

Come in, come in and join us . . . for your bones, treats and kisses

Our Tiny Tim was not here and for this we were sad

But he took Sarah with him and for this we were glad

(just kidding Sarah)

Mama got her new laptop early so at dawn she played

On Facebook she went, where she stayed and she stayed

Dennis slept in with dreams of fishing in his head

Cosmo the cat dreamed right along with him, near the end of the bed

Christmas dinner will be prime rib and his favorite of lobsters

As the kids are not here we get to splurge like big fat mobsters

I looked up the chimney, and didn't see St. Nick's behind

But he must have been here for there are gifts of many kinds

Today will be filled with thoughts of our family and friends

Of those serving our country, and standing to defend

We wish you all peace, joy and merriment today

And hope you remember it was the birth of Jesus that caused us to say

Merry Christmas to all and God Bless us come what may

(Written Christmas 2010 but wanted the kids to have this for future giggles!)

EACH ONE TELLS A STORY

Each one tells a story. Each one represents a time in our lives where laughter and love surrounded us and would not let us go. There is Tim and Sarah's "baby's first Christmas". The ceramic bears that I bought one year and painted our names on. Tim's was a bear holding a football, Sarah's was a girl bear holding her name on a sign, and ours were two bears "holding each other". Each year a new one, each year one to represent another part of our lives lived. Yes, each Christmas ornament told its own story and it always started and ended with . . . love.

There were the funny moments and memories that called for an ornament so special and so unique that there was no way you could forget. Sarah was called "Chub-a-choo" as in "Picachu" (no it was not an insult, it was a term of endearment between Dennis and Sarah), so our largest piece hanging on our tree each year is a big yellow Picachu. We laugh every time we take it out of the box. There is the child's uneven handwriting on a precious hand-painted one that Sarah made just for Dennis. He always smiled at this one special every time I held it up and never said a word. It was made with love.

In the summer of 2007, the kids came to stay with us for their summer visitation. They never went back to Buffalo as on Dennis' birthday (6/10/2008) we were awarded full custody. A large silver "2007" hangs on our tree as a reminder of all the celebration and hope we shared for our new start together.

The dogs each have their own. We have lab pups of all colors on our tree as we do in our home. Mocha and Molson each have a "puppy's first Christmas" ornament as I am a "MOM" to all babies, even the ones with fur. The cat is represented with a stuffed kitten holding a mouse. Each one brings a smile, each one a flood of memories, each one a piece of our lives that we will cherish forever.

There are ones to show his love of fishing, my love of crafts, the kid's favorite activities at different times in their lives. There are the ones that were given to me from co-workers. The ones made by the kids in school. There's a wooden one with his name carved across it that I ordered in August of 2011, but it came later in the year and he never got to see. It will always hang on our tree.

As we put our ornaments on the tree this year we will be sure to add something for the U.S. Army, something for "SENIORS" which I will let Grandma and Sarah argue over whether it represents Mom's longevity or Sarah's last year in high school. I have found an ornament that is a clear glass globe and inside is a miniature house in the woods. This house has all I ever dreamed "our house in the woods in the Carolinas" would be. In front of this home stands a yellow lab type dog (of course). It is perfect, it makes me smile, it makes me think of times we had and times we will never have again.

I know you do the same. I know you have your own box of memories that you unwrap each year and hang with smiles and maybe even a tear. It is how we remember, it is how we cherish and keep tiny sparkles of time glittering in our hearts. It is how we celebrate all that Christmas is . . . the birth of Jesus Christ, a time to celebrate, worship and treasure what each beautiful ornament represents to us . . . a colorful, glittering, sparkling, hand-crafted, timeless piece of . . . love.

CHANGING MY WORLD

Since Dennis has passed I have used the words "larger than life" more than once to describe all that he has meant to us. But physically speaking he was a big strong man, 5'10" and over 200 lbs. He had broad shoulders and these arms that I jokingly said "weighed 30 lbs. each" when he tossed them over me and cut off my airway as I slept. While he was a large framed man, we used to laugh because his hands were no bigger than mine. I have long thin (this being one of the only thin things on my entire body) fingers. We would put our hands up against each other and they were the same size. He hated his "short fat fingers" as he called them as they always inhibited his ability to get into the small places and fix equipment at work. I, on the other hand, loved his hands and how they reached for mine when we got out of the truck and walked into a store. How he would always rub my back gently and instinctively as we stood and talked to others. How when I would lay my head on his chest to sleep, he would cover my hand with his as we drifted off.

Yes, he was a presence when he walked into a room, a man of stature. He had deep set green eyes, coal dark silky black hair of which only two were gray. I found this highly odd and extremely unfair, as I seemed to be turning grayer by the moment. I convinced him in our early years to grow a moustache/beard combo and I cringed each time he shaved it off. Dennis was so handsome, and in my eyes he was big, burly, extremely strong, beyond funny, very sexy, and all man.

He used to think because he "didn't wear a smile" like some folks did, others didn't or wouldn't like him. I assured him each day they did, it just took them a little more time to get to know the man that I knew and loved. His exterior was a little intimidating and "Tony Soprano like." I promised him that if he spoke like the rest of the "Carolinians" and said "How are you doing today Ma'am?" instead of a New York accent and "You talkin' to me?" his big heart and fabulous sense of humor would shine through no doubt.

When I first laid eyes on Dennis I am sure there were fireworks going off in the room. (Ok maybe they were just going off in my head . . . either way they were loud and hard to ignore.) There was this thing that stirred in my heart that said, pay close attention to this man, do not look away when he speaks, go find out what he is all about. He was just magical to me. When he spoke I heard intelligence and a man who knew what he wanted. I heard strength, I heard a man who wasn't going to back down or back away from anything or anyone that got in his way. Mr. Determination. Mr. No Fear. This I admired. Yet when he looked at me and spoke "to me" his heart was in his eyes. Oh those eyes. A look could melt my heart and weaken my knees. He was gentle and sweet; (did I mention sexy? OK, sorry kids I think I did) cocky and arrogant, but loving at the same time. I knew I knew I knew . . . he was "the one" and I knew that meeting him **had forever changed my world.**

After we had been seeing each other for a while there came this weekend that he had to do his "Navy Reserves" duty. This weekend was different however in the fact that he wouldn't be coming home at the end of each day as he otherwise would have. For weeks and months (and each time I came over) I asked and begged for him to let me "work my magic" on his bachelor pad. I was dying to give it a "woman's touch". While I thought beer signs, Dale Earnhardt and Buffalo Bills memorabilia were "all the rage" I somehow felt that Dennis needed to emerge as a more sophisticated and mature man and he was definitely ready for a "new style". He finally gave in to my pleadings (as he always did) and gave me $100.00, which by the way was "a lot" of money for the times and for us. He said, "If you can *"change my world"* with $100.00, great, if you can't then at the very least could you make the front room not look like someone threw up Pepto-Bismol in there?" (His eloquent turn of a phrase!) Ok, Dennis, it's on. I accept your challenge.

This "front room" to which he referred was literally just that, the room at the front of the house. It was long but not wide; you came through the front door walked to the end of the room through another doorway that was adorned on each side by built-in bookshelves. Nobody really used this room but it was the first thing you would see when entering his home and it gave you an idea of what was to come. Of course he had to give that one last bit of instruction . . . "And don't, I repeat don't take down one Dale Earnhardt sign or this relationship is over". (Note to self . . . if he ever really ticks you off!)

I assured Dennis that while I held his love for *all things #3* sacred, it was really more the "hot pink" used by his last girlfriend that I was intent on "updating" to something a bit more, oh shall we say less "seriously was that color on clearance?"

My Mother was living with me at the time. I enlisted her help. We knew all about home improvement projects, we had done hundreds of them over the years. We were women on a mission. We had a plan. We made a list and checked it twice. We visited the Salvation Army, thrift stores, "everything is a $1 but really isn't" stores, and picked up things like fake grape vines, old stylish bottles, antique watering cans and picture frames, a small table stand and lamp, and a very pretty mantel clock. Then it was off to the paint store where we purchased 2 gallons of the most neutral light eggshell color we could find. We washed down walls, removed the entire Encyclopedia Britannica set from the shelves, and the bravest thing we did was lift the old ugly shag carpet to discover the prettiest hard wood floors underneath. We worked sun up to sun down. We scraped, scrubbed, washed, waxed, detailed and decorated.

When Dennis returned home at the end of his military weekend, we were waiting patiently yet with so much excitement for the familiar squeak of the front door. He came through that door and stopped dead in his tracks. He looked wide-eyed and amazed at how his room had been transformed. How it was now shelves full of personal touches. How far his $100 had really been stretched. How he was standing on the most beautiful hard wood floor that he didn't even know had existed a mere 48 hours before. The old was new; the mundane was modern and yes the "pepto-pink" was **Thank you Jesus,** gone!

He stood there and stared for the longest time. As no words were spoken we did the same but we were watching his face as to capture his full reaction. When the smile started to emerge, when his eyes became glassy, when the whisper of "Wow" escaped his lips, when he grabbed me and hugged me tight and said**, "Babe this is amazing and now this finally looks like a HOME."** It was then I knew. I knew I had accomplished more than I had set out to do. I knew that I may just have "**changed his world**" for the first time as well.

JANUARY 2012

(Facebook daily posts)

To Begin Again

JANUARY 1:

Again time will not slow down Dennis. It is already no longer the YEAR that you passed in. That is gone and now you passed "last year." I cannot believe this or get my head around it. I hold you so close in my heart and I think of you each day, all throughout the day. I am getting stronger and want you to watch me this year because I have a plan and yes of course, I am taking you along for the ride.

JANUARY 2:

I know not everyone on my list is as strong in their faith as others and we certainly do not all have the same beliefs. I am ok with that. I was not put on earth to judge. I personally believe in Jesus Christ as my savior and I KNOW that the Holy Spirit is in me working on me every day. How do I know? I can feel it and everything that runs through my being tells me this is true. So with that said, when this happens you can't help but want to share. That's how it works folks. Also I know a few other things . . . 1/ when you don't have the Holy Spirit working in you or you have not taken the time to read the Bible, sometimes other people talking about God and religion makes you uncomfortable. I was there. 2/ FB is not the pulpit but FB is to share ourselves with our friends and this is now a part of ME. 3/ I never ever wish to offend others so I will use FB appropriately on this subject matter. I am saying all of this because I am in a huge transformation in my life right now and I do not believe that this is just a phase because Dennis died. I believe that God is helping me through this yes, but he is also preparing me for Chapter 2 of my life. I am so ready to read that chapter and I hope you are all open minded enough to share the coming days ahead with me.

JANUARY 2:

Dear Dennis:

I was talking to "The Fish Guy" today and he took "Denny & Debbie" and will be placing them in a new home. They have outgrown our tank and were getting a little fishy-pissy you might say. Anywho . . . we now have 35 (yes 35) new fish that are now shackin' up with 2 of your originals. It's very pretty this fish condo and I know you would just love it. I did this for you. It's kind of a Memorial for you but no one knows that's why I still have it and have paid this man to make it beautiful and clear and attractive. Soon we will be bringing home "Baby Alley" and my goal is to see if she will live for 16 years like her Grand-pa-pa (Mr. Al G. Fish) did. You are loving this aren't you Dennis? Me your "fish abused wife". I knew you would. Love you darlin'.

JANUARY 3:

Missing Dennis today bad.

JANUARY 4:

Want to hear something funny? Back when we were waiting for the Coroner to call us back about Dennis' autopsy, Sarah was being silly and she answered the phone. Apparently the lady's cell was cutting out so when Sarah couldn't hear her she thought she had hung up . . . sooooooooooo . . . Sarah starts talking with a BRITISH ACCENT and saying, "Hello sometimes I like to pretend I am British" and "pip pip cheerio." After she spent two minutes at that the Coroner cut back in and said, "Can I speak to Debra Blood please?" OMG . . . . How do you go from laughing like an idiot to being somber to hear what I was about to hear? It was a true SARAH JANE moment.

JANUARY 5:

What I wouldn't give to have you come through the door at the end of the day.

JANUARY 8:

Dear Dennis:

As I dropped Timothy off for his 2nd day of Army drill I thought how proud you would have been. I just hope and pray that somehow you really know. Some say that the dead don't see on earth because if they could it could bring them sorrow and there is no sorrow in heaven. Well if that is the case, then I request about a trillion heaven minutes with you when I get there just to bring you up to speed. I miss you soooooooooooooooo much !!!

We all do.

JANUARY 9:

I miss you Dennis . . . but somehow I feel you loving me from all the way up there . . . (or 3 feet off the earth's surface as Sylvia Browne would say!! ha). Where ever you may be please know I think about you all day long. WE are getting stronger and WE are making you proud, promise.

JANUARY 9:

I am so very blessed. Thank you Lord !

JANUARY 10:

Dear Dennis:

I owe so much to you !!! ♥-n-u always

JANUARY 11:

Dear Dennis:

I miss my mornings starting with me bringing you your cup of coffee, you saying "come here and MOOSE ME (hug me)" and the smell of your cologne as you get ready for work.

JANUARY 11:

Dear Dennis:

Unless you have lost someone you love you don't know this feeling that seems to pull your heart down in your chest. Just when I think it's getting better another wave hits me. A flash of a past moment, you telling one of your silly jokes, you hugging me, us giggling like we did and even our fights that somehow we laughed about in the end. Are you up there smiling 24/7 "heaven time" because that is not how it goes down here. When will this end? When I see you again? When? I am sick of missing you . . . Is it ok to say that? I just want to be past this feeling, and thinking of you with only smiles and not tears. I guess we have a little ways to go yet honey. I love you.

JANUARY 12:

Since we pretend God reads FB, I can pretend that Dennis does too. Ha !

Dear Dennis:

Yesterday I was having a really bad missing YOU day. Today is better, it's totally up and down. I wonder if you miss me too. I think you loved me heart and SOUL as I did you, and since it's your SOUL that is up there I was praying for the possibilities. When the light of day shines and the tears clear I can see forward progress and healing, it's just sometimes those clouds roll in, you know? Good or bad days—I love you with all my heart each and every day I breathe.

JANUARY 14:

Life is so strange sometimes . . . Dennis used to call me up when we were young and in-love and play Bob Seger's, "Someday lady you'll accompany me". Tonight as a friend and I were driving by the Bi-LO Center they were getting ready for the BOB SEGER CONCERT !!!! That just seemed like a strange moment to think the closest I would ever get to Bob, would not be in Michigan where we were both from and where I should have seen him years ago, yet it would be at a moment in my life when I was the furthest from Dennis I had ever been.

JANUARY 15:

IN MEMORY OF YOU . . .

New blooms of rose pedals were yellow my friend

Delicate yet bold, brighter red as we neared the end

Most brought joy

Some brought tears

All moments were cherished, because they were ours to share through the years

There were regrets, challenges and growing pains

Tears of joy, sounds of laughter, losses and gains

You said I was loving, forgiving and one of a kind

Yet you rose up, gave your heart for two children, when nowhere else they would find

Never letting each other down, holding each other up, our plan always so clear.

We struggled to be "you and me", when being "US" we held so very dear

I said forever, I do, until death do us part

You said forever won't be long enough, but I will remain in your heart

I said we will grow old, side by side, you and me

You said just enjoy the ride darlin' for that's not meant to be

You stood in front of us to protect by our side each moment to share

You now watch from above still telling us you care

I don't know how it happened

I wasn't ready that day

But God came near, he called your name, HE led you his way

Each decision, each turn, each new day still echoes of you

Love built on friendship, blessed by God, intertwined hearts, what a fortunate two

It is with pride and grace I stand tall against this pain

I busy myself with tasks of new, teaching them to fly and honoring your name

I know what you taught me, what you did for us, what God sent you here for

I carry your words, your love, your strength as I near heaven's door

When you see me again Dennis, welcome me home as I did you each day

Take me in your arms, hold me close, together forever we will stay

JANUARY 16:

My son asked for 2 different things at 2 different times. I said NO to both and he knew that would be the answer before he asked. He left the room after the second time and I said, "Ok, why don't you try for 3 but THINK about what I am going to say before you ask . . . it's pretty simple and you KNOW Dennis would have said more than NO if he were here.". So he leaves my room, a couple of minutes later he walks back in (I can hear his footsteps in the hall and I know Tim) . . . I was holding my IPAD with a picture of Dennis up in front of my face and the minute he hit the door I tried to make a Dennis voice and I said, "NO !!!!" Tim looked at the picture and said, "He wouldn't have looked like that when he said NO like that!" So, I went to the next picture, held it up and said NO !!, Tim shook his head again and said, "No he would not have looked like that !" . . . I get to the next picture and it is of Dennis standing in front of the Earnhardt gate at Bristol Motor Speedway. DEAD SERIOUS LOOK, FULL BODY SHOT, ARMS CROSSED, AND STARING THAT DENNIS STARE !!! I held it up in front of my face, *started* to say "NO" and Tim yells, "YEP THAT'S IT, I GOT IT, THE ANSWER IS NO !!!!" We laughed ourselves silly !!!

JANUARY 17:

MLK Jr. was 39 yrs. old when he passed. Look at the legacy he left behind in that very very short time. That took compassion, courage, strength, determination and faith. What is your legacy? Is the world better for having had you in it? It's something we should all ask ourselves and then start making the changes however so little so the answer will be YES. Personally I DO NOT WANT to get to heaven's gates and have to say, "Hey thanks for those 70 some years down there . . . oh what did I do while there to show you that I was grateful? Ummmmm . . . let me think . . ."

JANUARY 18:

Dear Dennis:

When I broke down the other day—what came out was, that you used to be my entire world, and now you are becoming a part of my past. You used to have my ENTIRE heart, and now I hear things like "you will always have A PLACE in your heart for him". These things make me feel like I am moving away from you with each day that passes and that makes me sad and angry. I wish I knew why it had to be you to leave that day. I won't know those answers until my time is done and until then, I wait, and I miss you and I pray you know truly how much I loved you. Always, Debra

JANUARY 18:

You need to be moving if you want God to show you which way to go.

JANUARY 19:

Tim took a friend out for dinner (wink) at the Outback. He came home and handed me a bag of food. It was GRILLED LOBSTER TAIL. When I asked him why he spent his money on ME and told him that he didn't have to do that he said, "I looked for your favorite Crab Legs but they didn't have it so I got this . . . and because I love you!". HOW SWEET IS HE I ASK YOU??? Girls . . . pay attention to how those boys treat their Mama, it's a big huge sign !!! I love you Tim.

JANUARY 20:

Ok, this "ain't right" but last night Miss SJB and I were having a conversation that I didn't finish because she was asking me personal questions about how many guys I have dated in my life. We were discussing some of the "long lists" that girls now a days have while still in high school. I started to very discreetly answer her questions about guys I had dated before and guess what happened? DENNIS' PICTURE ON TOP OF THE DRESSER FELL OVER (forward when it was leaning back)! ! I said (to him), "OK, So NOW you decide to show yourself? That pissed you off huh baby? You know you are my ONLY LOVE!" lol. We got a real kick out of this.

JANUARY 20:

While talking to a very dear friend, I was told "Well, Debra, you may have missed your calling." With that she said "grief counselor". I thought about that and looking back here was my take. I have suffered through divorce, death of a spouse, a custody battle, being cheated on (not by Dennis), suicide, loss of a parent, and yet somehow God made me to get up each day, put on my big girl panties (as seen in a previous video—ha), find something to laugh about and while trying to heal myself hopefully serve as an inspiration to others. My point (besides the one on the top of my head) . . . THAT WHICH DOES NOT KILLS US ONLY MAKES US STRONGER !!! We can either sit down, cry and feel sorry for ourselves and NOT get back up . . . or we can make something good out of something heartbreaking and horrible!!! You know what I choose . . . how about you?

JANUARY 22:

Me and Tim-Tim went to the track. He ran, I walked and we did the touching of hands as he lapped me. Ha. Who would have ever thought I would be exercising with my son.

JANUARY 22:

Thought of you today and smiled. Miss you so much honey.

JANUARY 24:

Today I had my first appt. at my new Dr. WHO I LOVE BY THE WAY . . . She said my thyroid is low so that is possibly why the weight is not coming off as it should be with all of this diet and exercise. She said, "you having trouble losing weight?" I said, "Was it my SIZE 4 that threw you?" I know . . . what a smarta$$ I am . . . but anyway we love each other now (of course) and I am so excited that I have a REAL DR. that cares, that is so good and so thorough. Those are so hard to find now-a-days !!

JANUARY 24:

Dennis—heard your ROLLING STONES driving this morning. I had a thought . . . have you seen Dale Earnhardt Sr. yet? I figured since you were his BIGGEST FAN that maybe God would let you have a few minutes with him to discuss all of those races!

JANUARY 24:

Whatever this is that makes me so damn happy all the time should be made into a pill, bottled and sold !!! I just have a hard time NOT smiling sometimes. I get on here and just LOVE my friends and all of their comments, I LOVE my family and that I get to watch "the next generation" grow, I LOVE how we lift each other up, act like dorks and don't care, support each other through death, loss of jobs, and just BAD days !!! Yes, I am high on life and annoying like that but this appears to be how God made me and YOU ARE STUCK WITH IT MY FRIENDS!

JANUARY 25:

On my phone we have a short video clip taken on 9/8/2011 Sarah's 16th birthday. It is of us singing Happy Birthday to Sarah. Dennis is on the video. He is singing in a nasally, high pitched, whinny voice and you can hear him through everyone else . . . it's pretty funny. Then the video goes to him and I think I said I was putting the video on Facebook and his expression changed immediately and he said, "No you are not!" It's so good to hear his voice and see his face. Makes me sad but I love it just the same.

JANUARY 25:

It's true, the Doctor asked me why I checked on the list of symptoms that my memory was getting worse and then she asked me how long this has been going on . . . you know what my answer was right?

JANUARY 25:

Dear Dennis:

When I used to wake up late in the night or the early hours of morning the first thing I did was listen for your breathing. It always brought me comfort and a peace knowing you were right by my side. Now I wake and pray that you are still by my side and can hear me breathing somehow. I miss you.

JANUARY 25:

Dear Dennis:

Today is 4 mos. since the day you were called home. I cannot believe it's been that long already. You know you were larger than life to us and this is such a great loss so we are doing the best we can. I can only imagine that you are busy helping out and setting up a place for all of us to gather when we are called. I love you so much sweetheart and while I heal a little more each day, I love you no less. Always, Debra

JANUARY 26:

DEAR MOTHER NATURE:

If you could quit making it RAIN long enough for me to walk outside my arse would be much smaller than it has been known to be in the past !!! This is getting old (and so am I) so hurry it up please. Thank you.

JANUARY 26:

On your way home from work today, try to recall all the reasons you fell in love with your other half . . . and when you get there . . . . hug them twice for each one of those things !!! Trust me on this one.

JANUARY 27:

I started to read this book about becoming "one" after losing your spouse and being a part of a couple and you know what I realized? I didn't need to read that . . . I have always been DEBRA, ME, ONE. Dennis and I loved each other very much, we were best friends and we were ALWAYS together, but we were very much DENNIS and DEBRA, individuals. Standing here today and looking back, while I miss US deeply I am grateful that I held onto ME, because that is who has to go forward each day.

JANUARY 27:

I am not the only one missing you honey, I sure hope you know.

JANUARY 28:

One of the things that I SO ADMIRED AND LOVED about Dennis was his intellect. He was so very smart. He read constantly and about many many different things and especially things he didn't know or understand. I used to joke and say, "OMG were you born knowing that?" when he could answer the most "out there question" in a moment's notice. I love books. They do open up a world to us that we can find by no other means. I am reading about SPIRITS now. Nothing ungodly just general "other side" information taken from those that claim to have "been there and back". It brings me peace to think my husband is busy, can reach out to us when he wishes, and while heaven is nothing but "love and forgiveness" he does not feel stress, anger, or hurt over anything from his past. It may seem crazy to some but this helps me move forward. Now then Dennis, since we have that out of the way . . . time to read about how to install tile!

JANUARY 30:

When I met Dennis' mom years ago (she passed in 1998) and I asked "what was Dennis like as a baby?" I will never forget she said, "he was one big ball of energy!". As I was reading about spirits and what happens to our souls after we pass from this earth it mentions that while we are no longer in our human-earthly-physical bodies . . . we are more so, "ONE BIG BALL OF ENERGY!!" See there my sweetie . . . from birth to death to eternal life . . . you have never changed! lol

JANUARY 30:

I fed the two guys that are doing some work on the house, chicken wing soup. One said, "if my wife kicks me out, can I come here, I love you !" hahahaha. Tim says "you know Mom, men love woman that can cook!" to which I replied, "Great Tim, maybe I will get my next husband at the Country Fair Chili cook off !!!"

MAMA BIG BOOBS

If you know me personally and have known me for some time the reasoning behind a name like "Mama Big Boobs" needs no explanation. If you don't know me personally or we have never met . . . well I think you have already caught on in just two sentences and I credit you with being a quick thinker.

You will see reading another chapter of this book called "What's in a name?" that my beloved had a great gift for giving nicknames to others, especially those that he loved. My name is Debra, but he loved to call me "Debbie" when he was conveying a message of affection. One of our favorite memories of "Debbie" comes from what became an almost expected response that Dennis would give to my cooking of dinner each night. As I have explained he loved his food. I was always the one that was teased by my family that I "couldn't boil water" without messing it up but over the years I honed my skills and while I was not necessarily on the same level as Julia Childs I could hold my own.

Each of us sat in the same place each night at the dinner table. Dennis was at the end at "the head of the table", Sarah at the other end and Tim and I would face each other across the table. More times than not Dennis would finish his meal and head to the front room to get caught up on his "paperwork" to finish out his work day. I enjoyed trying out new recipes and making it my goal to ensure that everyone enjoyed each meal and we didn't get bored with the "same ole' same ole'". If at the end of the meal Dennis got up and walk passed me, patting my back and saying "Great job there Debbie!" I knew I had done well and reached my goal. If at the end of the meal he stood and walked passed me with no touch or pat, then we all came to take this as an indication that the evening menu was just "alright". It got to the point where my "scorecard" for cooking was based on this little ritual of his patting my back. If I put a lot of time and effort into a recipe, was all excited for everyone to test it in hopes of raving reviews and I **didn't** get a pat on the back and a "Debbie" remark . . . well then my hopes were dashed until the next time. Sarah and I still recall the night it played out just this way. I had spent hours on a new recipe, followed it exact, and when no pat came to me on his way around the table, we both yelled, "Heyyyyyyyyyyyyyyyyyyy???? It was good !!! Get back here!" I am not sure he understood all that we read into his little "pats of love" but we watched for them daily.

Ok back to the boobs (ha). I have never been a "small" woman. Big boned was always a nice way of saying that there was much of me to love. Dennis, like any typical man had his "rathers". He'd "rather" see a woman who wore anything that said "Double D" than did not. Are you with me? I know he loved my eyes as he always told me they were beautiful, and I believe he thought my hands to be "delicate and pretty." I can tell you however for a fact that the part of my body that he adored the most was once a "meal provider" to my children as babies.

At some point in time he decided that "Mama Big Boobs" was his new pet name for me. I want to say it started when I had the kids on his lap and was trying to take a picture of them together. Instead of yelling, "say cheese" he loudly exclaimed, "Say Mama Big Boobs" which got the biggest laugh and smiles ever, because what young pre-teen child does not giggle excessively over the word "boobs" right?

On it went from there. You could hear him call this name out when I was in the bedroom and he and the kids were all getting ready to watch a movie and wanted me to join them. Maybe if he was anything but their "Step-Dad" he would not have taken such liberties, but it was always done to bring a smile about and for that we never discouraged his humor. To this day the kids still share that their Step-Dad "used to tell us that Mom married him for his big . . . (pause) . . . Wallet!" When you hear Sarah laugh hard and say, "I don't think he was really talking about his wallet", well I guess you know his mission had been accomplished.

It is with all of this said I need to share with you to what extent my husband took his love for this silly nickname he had bestowed upon me. It was just a couple of years ago and it was my birthday. He had bought tons of crab legs, potatoes, corn on the cob and was doing a big crab boil for the occasion. This was not a surprise as I have shared many times that crab legs were my favorite food and my "traditional birthday meal". This particular year however he decided that he was going to give me a "special" birthday cake. He came to me and said, "Sarah and I are running out for a little bit and we will be back, no questions". Ok, it was my birthday, I was excited as to what this would mean, so agreed, no questions. An hour went by, no Dennis and Sarah. Two hours go by, no Dennis and Sarah. Three . . . ok now I am getting a little worried. I broke the "no questions" rule and called his cell. Yes, they were fine, but no they were not done and yes they would "be home soon, no questions Debra!"

If was after the crab legs, potatoes, and corn was all gone. After the table had been cleared, the lights went out and I was told to "close your eyes" that I knew the cake was on its way. When I opened my eyes to them singing "Happy Birthday" and I looked down what I saw was a cake with what on it? You got it! BIG BOOBS! My cake said, "Happy Birthday Mama Big Boobs" AND had cupcakes representing the female form. My favorite part was when the kids would have normally asked for the piece that had the "flower" or whatever was the biggest part of the cake decoration, this was where Dennis looked at me and let me know without words just exactly "which part" he was hoping for. Now I ask you who else could claim they had such a cake?

After we cut into the cake (or boobs) and the giggling finally died down, Sarah and Dennis went on to explain that the reason they were gone for so long that day was because they had driven all over God's creation to find those pink, coconut covered snowball cupcakes to use for the "boobs" as it had to be perfect.

They were on a mission they were. In all of its craziness, I know it was a true mission of love.

FEBRUARY 2012

(Facebook daily posts)

Discovery

FEBRUARY 1:

There are things that we don't want to happen but have to accept, things we don't want to know but have to learn, and people we can't live without but have to let go. ~ Author Unknown

FEBRUARY 2:

Alright Dennis, you always said I was smart so here is the plan. I am taking your stock in Philips making enough $ to publish my book, then make millions on the book circuit and my appearances on Ellen and the Today show! lol. Are you buying this? If I pull this off you will be stomping on clouds with excitement I know!

FEBRUARY 2:

Not a day goes by that I don't think of you and all that we shared. Always, Debra

FEBRUARY 3:

I was asked yesterday by someone that only knows me in passing, "do you think you will ever remarry" I said, "Well, you know . . . I put my ad up on Match.com but it appears that there is no big need for a middle aged overweight woman, with 2 teens, 4 dogs, 1 cat, a 90 yr. old Mother and a tank full of fish, BUT I'LL GET BACK TO YOU ON THAT!!!"—Now let's go back to he only "knew me in passing" because if he had KNOWN ME he would have seen that answer coming a mile away !!!! lol

FEBRUARY 3:

My brain is a little bit fried tonight. I was a high finance woman today. Geesh Dennis you would have been so proud. I talked to a broker about stocks and I think I carried my own through the conversation. Then I got Dennis' retirement into an Annuity to earn while we are waiting for me to become a classy old broad !!! I did the research, I prayed, I asked tons of???, and then I went for what I felt was right. That's all you can do I believe. Well besides channel your dead husband.

FEBRUARY 4:

When I wake at 2 a.m. alone and missing you when I hear "GOLD DUST WOMAN" by Fleetwood Mac driving down the road and smile at how this could be the favorite song to such a BLACK SABBATH fan, when I see myself reading about stocks and "getting it", when I find the right tool for the job that I would have never thought I could do, when I say something that rings of discipline with love mixed in, when I look at the calendar of life events that will be here and gone before I can blink . . . . it all says Dennis, it all says you once were here and we were once very much US and very much in love, and young and starting out with such excitement and such big goals. I will never forget you ever! Always, Debra

FEBRUARY 4:

I started up Dennis' old computer (and just for the record I am pretty proud of myself that I "cracked the password code" by "thinking like my husband") and opened up Outlook and there was an email in this sent file from him to my email address (that I swear I don't remember) that says. "testing, testing, darling . . . 123, if you get this you have just been emailed by one hell of a guy you lucky woman you love ya". That was my silly man! lol

FEBRUARY 4:

Tim & I were just on our way home and WAR PIGS came on (totally a Dennis song). Tim lit up my phone with Dennis' pic as my screensaver and then bounced my phone up/down, back and forth so DENNIS WAS "HEAD BANGIN" HA. Funny kid!

FEBRUARY 5:

I can remember being around people before that have lost a spouse and you always feel uncomfortable bringing "them" up for fear that you will make the person upset. But what I can tell you from being on this side of things . . . I never want to be anywhere that I don't feel comfortable enough to talk about Dennis or share a moment or story of our lives together. Keeping his memory alive is so important to me and makes my heart feel better because it keeps him with me. I know that I will move on and someday I may love again but he was just too important to not remember and share with others. So, Thank you to all of my friends who were here for me this week and listened or held on at just the right moment.

FEBRUARY 7:

God says do your good works in silence, in other words you don't go "do and brag" so I hope this is not taken as such, I just have to share this. I was at Wal-Mart today and the man in front of me laid a loaf of bread, box of spaghetti, can of sauce, sm. bag of meatballs, milk, and a few other items. He had smiled at me and nodded and said, "ma'am". I just got the sense he was a nice, sincere man who might have been a little down on his luck. I don't know what my full take was but I was starting to get this feeling of worry the longer he counted his money and "change". He moved ahead a few inches and asked the cashier to wait while he continued to count. I moved my head in front of the screen and it said $29.45. I motioned to the cashier with my card that I was going to swipe it and she nodded. He continued to count change and not notice what we were doing. She handed me the receipt and I tapped him on the shoulder and said, "Sir, here. Your items are paid for . . . have a good day." Well, let me tell you what . . . he started to cry, he said he has been without a job for nearly a year and he has all he can do to feed his family and he was so grateful. He asked for my name and I said, "No Sir, you don't get that, you get this" (pointing to his groceries). Now my point in sharing this is this . . . WE DO NOT KNOW BY LOOKING AT ANYONE IF THEY ARE POOR, RICH, HOMELESS, GOOD, EVIL OR OTHERWISE . . . AND I don't think God wants us to make our decision to help others solely on what WE THINK WE SEE. I personally am blessed that I could help him and his family and that was my reward. I think of all the love and support and blessings I have had since I lost the man that I loved more than life itself and how I will ever pay that back I don't know . . . but maybe this is it . . . one act of kindness at a time. Give it a try there is nothing that will make you feel better I promise! Thanks for listening.

FEBRUARY 7:

Dear Dennis:

Today was a good day. I had no calls from school nurse, nobody broke a hip, had a seizure, got detention, jumped a fence . . . it was amazing !!! I had an opportunity to do as God taught us to do and I seized the moment and without thinking twice, call me crazy but I felt a little closer to you somehow. I sold $34.00 in jewelry to help two beautiful girls help others around the world. I also did my 2nd day at Curves . . . there is an older woman there with the body of a 20 yr. old and you just keep watching from that view of yours honey . . . . I am on my way (careful now you can't make remarks about my backside up there in front of the big guy !! Not cool !!) I miss you so much and love you with all my heart !!! P.S. You can tune out while I do my first Zumba class. I feel as though you will laugh so hard it may cause an earthquake out in California. Always, Debra

FEBRUARY 8:

Yesterday I got the SWEETEST message from one of the kid's friends. I won't name names but I was VERY touched and the last line made me giggle, so (of course) had to share.—

To Sarah and Timmy's Mom: I just want to say that your posts and statuses are inspiring and always make me smile and give many outlooks in my life and I bet I'm not the only one to think that. You are an amazing role model and are very strong for your family. I have never seen such an amazing and funny mom. I wouldn't be offended if you gave my mom pointers, haha

FEBRUARY 8:

Ok, I remember when I thought the theme to the Titanic by Celine Deon was a sweet song . . . now that I hear it and you are gone it takes on a whole new meaning and it makes driving a little bit harder to accomplish! My heart will go on Dennis . . . with you in it.

FEBRUARY 8:

Check this out. I just read this in an exercise magazine—"Loneliness increases the risk of obesity, cancer and premature death. A study of MICE from Ohio State (that explains a lot said the Michigan girl) University showed that social stimulation helped the animals convert energy storing white fat to energy burning brown fat. Consequently, the animals lost weight. Researchers achieved greater social interaction by housing 15 to 20 animals together rather than in individual cages. If these results apply to HUMANS, you should strive for MORE SOCIAL INTERACTION RATHER THAN COMMUNICATING WITH PEOPLE ON THE COMPUTER."******* I AM SORRY DID THEY JUST SAY I AM FAT BECAUSE I FACEBOOK TOO MUCH?

FEBRUARY 9:

Dear Dennis: My how life changes hey? Tonight I am going to Curves (Day #4) as I continue my quest to be that super hot sexy woman that I have always dreamed of being. Then to H&R Block to get our taxes done. Remember when life was easy and we did them ourselves because really how hard was it to report $8.50 an hr.? Then off to my 17th grocery visit for the week, which you hated and said wouldn't happen if I had only made a list. Well, sweetie that's a nice theory but . . . no. Then it's more jewelry making, some laundry, dinner for the family and SLEEP! Tell me about your day Dennis, are you up there floating on clouds watching all of this busy business down here? Miss you my love, Always Debra

FEBRUARY 10:

Dear Dennis:

Let's talk taxes, you wanna? Remember how they say the only two things certain in life are death and taxes, APPARENTLY this year I am the POSTER CHILD for truth in advertising so to speak. The good news is we don't have to pay those (IRS) folks but what you have to pay just to get to the point to know if you have to pay is a bit painful in and of itself. I can't become an expert in Stocks, gutter hanging, mechanics, fish tank maintenance AND taxes, while taking care of Mom, two kids, 4 dogs, 1 cat and a house and somehow make time to get my CURVES on !!! So this whole idea that I am going to assume all of the knowledge that you possessed to make up for you not being here is starting to give me "sharp stabbing pains" through my cranium. So, here is the deal . . . I was wondering if you would mind sending me "mental knowledge waves" please? You know, you see me struggling with something, you gather the info, and you shoot it through the clouds from your spirit to mine! Why not? We got that kind of connection right? K—you work on that while I go try to figure out what that noise is coming from the garbage disposal, ugh !!! Missing you each second of each minute of each day . . . Always, Debra

FEBRUARY 10:

Since 9.25.2011 I have become ultra-sensitive to many things. I hear words to songs more now than before, I notice older couples holding hands and think (they have been blessed with time). Driving down the road I heard . . . "Even though we ain't got money, I'm so in love with you honey . . ." which took me back to days at Treemont St., where we shoved the couches (that we bought for $40 each at the Salvation Army—no lie !) together, made our own pizza out of flour, water, yeast, etc. (yes kids that is how it's done), watched non-stop movies and didn't emerge until Monday morning ! It was just us being happy for we didn't know what we didn't have and if we did it didn't matter . . . because we had each other. I am so grateful for my memories of us !

FEBRUARY 10:

Ok I met someone that knew my husband! How shocking and exciting at the same time. AND,. They loved him and described him as smart, and so funny and told me how incredibly well liked he was. It made me sad, it made me smile, it made me proud !!! I miss you Dennis—you were such an amazing person !!!

FEBRUARY 13:

Wow Dennis, I hope you are watching as you have one friend who has done more than step up in your memory!

FEBRUARY 13:

Dear Dennis:

Missing you does not begin to cover it today. Always, Debra

FEBRUARY 14:

Talked to Dennis' Aunt Elaine last night. I love her. It makes me miss him more but at the same time it is like bringing him near.

FEBRUARY 14:

True Story. The first gift Dennis ever gave me was a heart diamond necklace (what a guy right?) anyway it was wrapped up in a BIG HEART BOX. Well just like a kid at Christmas I was almost more intrigued with the box. I told him I would save it forever (and I did !! of course). He said, "Ok, Debbie (what he called me when being a smarta$$) let's make a deal . . . you save that heart box forever (and you will) and when I forget to get you something on Valentine's Day (and I will) . . . you take that box out and jump up and down with happiness and thank me all over again!" lol. Nice try big guy !!!

FEBRUARY 14:

Matthew 5:4

Blessed are those who ***mourn***, for they will be ***comforted***.

♥ . . . and without asking . . . God sent a special friend to me this morning to bring me comfort as I mourned. I believe.

FEBRUARY 14:

Whew !!! I did it. I made it through LOVE day without my love. I went to Curves (yay me !), then on the way home I was pushing the buttons on the radio because every song sucked and as I pulled into our subdivision there it was . . . GIMME SHELTER by The Rolling Stones . . . his favorite Stones song. Thanks for riding home with me Dennis . . . that did make it better !!! Love you so.

FEBRUARY 14:

Sarah said, "Mom what did you and Dennis do last year for Valentine's Day?" Well, we ate something chocolate for dessert, he TOLD ME ABOUT the card that he was going to buy me BUT DIDN'T and then said, "but that's ok, cause I love ya' Debra Blood!" Yep, that was our love day !!! It was so us.

FEBRUARY 15:

Sarah and I were laughing last night at how Dennis used to say, "You are a NERD DEBRA BLOOD!" ha. (He loved to use my FULL NAME whenever he spoke to me). Anyway in 5 minutes or less we listed the 25 top things he did that truly made him KING OF THE NERDS! It was good to miss him and laugh instead of miss him and cry.

FEBRUARY 15:

I know you are near. I love you. Nite sweetheart.

FEBRUARY 16:

(Jesus said:) "I am the resurrection, and the life: he that believeth in me, though he were dead, yet shall he live: And whosoever liveth and believeth in me shall never die." (John 11.25-26)—This is how I know Dennis is truly ok.

FEBRUARY 16:

Honesty is best. I didn't want to go to Curves today. My shoulders and neck and upper back (hurt everyday my entire life) but today they really hurt. I laid down for about 30 minutes at lunch and that helped, and then nearing 4 p.m. all I could think was "I don't want to exercise I want to go to bed". Did I? NO. I walked up to Sarah and said, "Let this be an example to you. The next time you don't want to do something remember this moment. I DO NOT, REPEAT DO NOT WANT to go to exercise but I AM GOING". So, how did it turn out? My goal was 200 points over all (remember yesterday I was happy with 161). Today . . . 206 !!!!! Damn straight !!!—Side note: As I was driving through the grocery parking lot afterwards, **my** U.S. Army Reserve son ran by me smiling as he did his PTs.

FEBRUARY 16:

For all of you out there that think I have forged on and hear me tell of big steps forward, call me amazing and think I have this grief thing mastered, let me share this with you as well. I can go for weeks and be fine and then a heaviness of shear depression hits me so hard I can hardly breathe and I am still thrown back to day one when they said he was gone. I miss him so bad it seems almost impossible that he is not really coming back—even now, months later when it should be more real. I will get through this so no I am not out jumping off a bridge while you read this (not to worry) but I just didn't want you to think that loss of this magnitude is handled by everyone in the same manner that I have chosen to handle it. We all grieve differently, and there are moments I don't share. I know you are shocked. There is a flood of tears that only those BFFs and the pups (ha) get to hear (lucky you guys) and I know in a year when many things about me have changed—my heart will still ache for him, I will still miss my best friend Dennis. So if I inspire you. I am grateful I can. If my strengthening faith moves you or turns you in another direction, I can only do what I feel is right, I am not perfect and I am not always strong and I certainly don't know the correct and easy way to lose a husband. I make a step forward and then crumble because he is not here to take the step with me. I do something to make him proud and want to come home and share it with him and can't. My pain effects my kids and everything about me. I just wanted you to see all sides of this ugly thing called grief. It's not pretty and I don't have it down to a science, I am just doing the best I can. Thanks for listening and always being here for me.

FEBRUARY 20:

I read this book and it was about a woman who drowned but then was brought back to life. Her claim is that she saw her daughter who passed before her and was told to "go back you are not done". Every book that is written from the perspective of someone who died and came back (so to speak) always says they "didn't want to come back to Earth". Always if given the choice, no matter who they were leaving behind, heaven was so full of peace, joy, and love they just didn't want to leave. I like to think that is exactly what my husband is experiencing now . . . never-ending peace, joy and love beyond measure.

FEBRUARY 21:

Dear Dennis:

Remember when I used to jokingly say HOME DEPOT makes me cry? That was just because it was not "MY" kind of place. Yesterday I was there and when I left it "literally" made me cry as I remembered it to be the last place you and I were at together before going home that morning. Little things like that throw me sometimes, which makes me wonder . . . if I had left that day instead of you, would you be crying in the parking lot of Hobby Lobby right now? I miss you honey and yes, I know this made you laugh.

FEBRUARY 21:

One of the most cherished memories I will EVER have . . . The day Dennis passed, (within an hour) on our way home from town, I was driving and I had my right hand on the seat. He reached over, grabbed my hand, very sincerely and very sweetly said, "you know I love you right?" I will always believe that while he may not have known that 9.25 was his last day . . . somehow he knew something. My answer that day . . . "I have never doubted it for a minute".

FEBRUARY 22:

It was weird . . . I pulled into the parking lot of the grocery store, I shut off the music and so there was this perfect sudden quiet moment and this feeling of warmth just came over me in a total rush. I know you think I have lost it but I simply said, "I love you too Dennis", and then it went away. I would bet his spirit is here with me. I was not thinking of him that I knew of at that moment and my mind was totally somewhere else. It was just a very surreal moment.

FEBRUARY 23:

Dear Dennis:

As I do something as simple as repaint and redecorate our bedroom I am caught in a "this was ours, it's now changing, and he won't see it" moment that hurts and causes me anxiety, yet I keep going. It's a struggle to move forward but NOT leave us behind, to ensure I don't allow myself to become stuck in the past but yet never wanting to be, do, have or experience anything without you. We shared EVERY moment, everything in our day and our lives. To not do that now feels so wrong and so strange at times. This whole "being a widow" thing SUCKS big time my love. So, when we talked about you going first is this what you meant when you used to say "Debra you will be FINE, I have no doubt?" Seriously dude, you had no idea what you were saying? Ugh. ♥ Love you my dear !! Always—Debra

FEBRUARY 25:

I missed you so many times today. Did you hear all the times I spoke to you while decorating the bedroom ! LOL. Were you having issues after I moved you like the 4th time in 20 mins. !! ha. I love you so much Dennis—I hope your peace is beautiful and you know I have your heart ♥

FEBRUARY 26:

Baby I live for the moment when every memory does not send a stab of pain through my heart and a tear down my face. I miss you all the time, but days like today . . . I miss you more !!

FEBRUARY 26:

The phone rang and it was Tim. Sarah answered, Tim asked for "Mom". Sarah said, "TIM she can't come to the phone right now because she is looking up men on Match.com". OMG my kids are funny!

FEBRUARY 26:

Dear Dennis: It's been a long day, but you lived it with me honey !! (Now that's talent I tell ya'). Nite baby . . .

FEBRUARY 26:

If you will not run when you feel fear, fear will run because it has seen faith.

FEBRUARY 28:

When I miss you the most I think, "if only I could hold you one more time", and when I pray the hardest and just listen with my heart I hear, "but you will".

FEBRUARY 28:

The sad part of memories is that no amount of remembering you will bring you back.

FEBRUARY 29:

When I say I miss you . . . it doesn't really explain the millions of ways or reasons why. If you were here right now we would be having dinner, but we know longer eat at 7 p.m. While I am starting to do ME things, I miss the US things so much. I miss hugging you at the end of every day as you come through the door, the way you would say "Hello Sarah" (In a Seinfeld "Hello Newman" sort of way) and call for Tim. Even how you greeted Mocha each night as she had to have some Dad time too. You left such a void in our lives Dennis and no amount of activity, events, stuff, trips or plans can fill that void. Missing you just seems so small and vague compared to the feeling it is meant to describe.

WHEN THE DAM BREAKS

I drive by a place that we loved to go, someone tells a joke that I think you would have totally cracked up over, an event happens and you miss it, a significant date comes and goes, our children come home with a problem that only you could fix, I burn dinner, the smell of your cologne as another man passes, leaves falling from the trees during "our favorite time" of the year which now signifies your passing. These things bring tears.

Just down the road (Saluda "Dam" Rd.) is the dam. You used to love to drive by there. At times you would stop and watch the water when it was high from days of rain. I used to say, "what if the dam breaks?" to which you said so matter of fact, "Have a little faith Debra, it won't".

Sometimes it's specific things with memories and feelings that run so incredibly deep. I heard the song "Sweet Melissa" the other day. Why did that bring tears? There would have been a little girl, with dark hair, green eyes, she would have smiled like me and looked like you; she would have called us Mom and Dad. When you passed she would have been a precious child who you would have called your youngest daughter. I carried her for three months and God took her home before we could see her or hold her. Our hearts were so broken that day it seemed impossible that we would ever be able to get up and function again as normal people do. You said, "Every little girl should have a song title like that with her name". I have lived years pushing her, that day, the pain you showed over that loss, and that memory so far back in my mind as to not live with that grief and to be able to move forward, yet now I shed tears wondering if you are with our "sweet Melissa", holding her hand, protecting and loving her as you did Sarah and Tim. Does she smile like me and look like you Dennis?

Sometimes I just get overly tired and weighed down with life decisions . . . and yes I get lonely and miss my best friend. It all pours out of my soul one tear at a time. I think the dam will break soon. How could it possibly hold from the weight of it all? But it doesn't. The dam doesn't break. Remarkably it remains strong and steadfast.

They say "that which does not kill us makes us stronger". Others watch you as you hold your head up high and proceed through the days after a loss. They see decisions you make. They see you taking care of your home, nurturing your children, working and paying the bills. They watch you making decisions they couldn't imagine making on their own. Yes, they see all of this and they think . . . "isn't she handling this so well . . . look how strong." All awhile inside you feel that if you could just take one more step in the always present cement before it dries you will have made progress. If you could just fill your lungs with a full breath of air without giving up at mid-inhale you could claim success. The tears just keep coming.

What makes me cry the most? Going to church and being close to God. Some might find that strange but the closer I am to God the closer I am to you Dennis and that makes my heart joyful and sad and just overwhelmed at times. You know, you and I never found a church that we wanted to call "home" since we moved to South Carolina. Now looking back it seems ironic to me that about a year before you died I began reading the Bible more and more. You questioned "the sudden interest", and I said it was more of a "delayed interest than sudden". Now I go and study the word of God and the entire time that I am reminded of his love for me, I am smiling because of his love for you.

I hear the preacher talk of God and his promises. He talks of salvation and Jesus. He talks of giving your life to Christ and never looking back so that someday when we are called home we can live in eternity together with those that have passed before us, and here comes the tears. I think, he's talking about us Dennis . . . he's talking about you and me. You are in that home, I am in this one, we are in two different worlds, I miss you, there are just no words to explain to what extent, and I don't know if you do or can miss me. Death is the only thing that one can do but can't tell someone else about first hand. Since the day we fell in love it's the only thing we haven't been able to do together, yet someday we will together experience the same thing.

I went back to my hometown in Michigan since you have died. I was with friends on a pontoon boat riding around the lake that I was so blessed to grow up on. None of this hit me as sad; none of this struck me as overwhelming, on the contrary I was so excited to be there. It was all beautiful and peaceful until I realized that we were floating directly in front of the house that you and I rented just last summer. I could see you standing there by the door way, I could see you standing on the dock with your fishing hat and Seminoles shirt on. My heart nearly seized up and the tears just instantly began to fall. Oh God how I miss you and the fun we had and the love you showed to me. You laughed at me because as soon as we got the keys, brought in the luggage, Timothy and I changed into our suits and raced to the water and then swam together to the raft, just like I did when I was a kid. When I told you of how much that moment meant to me, to be able to relive a childhood joy with my 17 year old son, you kissed my forehead and pulled me into your chest with that big arm, flashed me that smile and I knew you were sincerely happy for me and what you had made possible.

As time goes by I pray that the tears will fall less, and the joy of the moments we shared will shine through more. While the tears are still falling, be it a drop at a time or a river rushing through . . . somehow I picture you and God on the other side of that dam, pushing against it with all of your might. I am "having a little faith" just as you said Dennis, no matter how high the water may rise.

MARCH 2012

(Facebook daily posts)

Time marches on

MARCH 1:

Thanks for the support these past few weeks. Some weeks are great and some weeks I miss Dennis so bad I can't seem to function properly. I know you want to start your day with smiles and reading my sadness may not be conducive to that end so I appreciate you hanging with me through all of this. It's now been 5 months. I can't believe it myself. I know I am stronger and have come a long way . . . and again I thank you for that.

MARCH 2:

I made a trip home to Jacksonville Florida this weekend. I didn't have much time and after I missed my exit and did a tour of GA I had even less time. I wanted to visit everyone but I promised my dear friend Dani that I would come and we would have some US time that we have not had in forever. It was all too short but it was great to see her husband and beautiful girls. Her oldest is beautiful, smart and funny and her youngest, well, she said "Miss Debra !!! and then . . . SHOT THROUGH THE HEART, YOU'RE TO BLAME . . . YOU GIVE LOVE . . . A BAD NAME !!" Taylor my love you are my little Bon Jovi buddy, I love you both !! I will have a longer weekend there soon (in FL) where I will visit all of my FL family and friends. I couldn't make myself go down memory lane and drive by our old home as that was just a little bit too painful right now. I have another story to share in another post.

MARCH 2:

Ok I have sinned. You know how I have said that Dennis is with me, protecting me, guarding me, etc. So, I kind of tried to put that to the test this weekend. I was stopped doing over 90 mph in a 70 in GEORGIA. Not the state to break that kind of law. So I had my husband's picture on the dash and when I saw the trooper the minute he saw me, we had this instant connection and I knew I was done for. I had to choose . . . lie or get a BIG TICKET. I pulled over and waited with the DL, registration and insurance in hand. Sarah and I broke into nervous laughter debating the choices between good and evil and when I saw him walk up it was a done deal . . . I said to Sarah under my breath . . . "be SAD". It went like this:

Trooper: Is there a reason you are in such a hurry?

Me: You wouldn't believe me if I told you.

Trooper: Try me

Me: I am on my way to Jacksonville for a memorial service for my husband and so far I have toured the entire state of Georgia because I missed my exit.

Trooper: Your husband died?

Me: Yes Sir

Trooper: and that's him? (Pointing to his picture on the dash)

Me: Yes Sir

Trooper: And is that your daughter? (Pointing to Sarah)

Me: Yes Sir

Trooper: Ok, I will take this into consideration and give you a warning.

He went back to his car to write the ticket.

Sarah says . . . "MOM !! What are we going to do (knowing we just lied) if he asks us how Dennis died."

My reply: WELL TELL THE TRUTH OF COURSE !!!!!! LOL

—Ok, ok, I know . . . using your dead husband is not all that charming, I get it AND surely I am not up for Mother of the Year, but hey . . . sometimes the guy on the shoulder not wearing the wings wins over.

The funny part is I really was lost for a while and because I told the Trooper that, he gave me directions to I-95 which was like a mile up the road. I wanted to yell, "Where were YOU A HOUR AGO WHEN I WAS IN BACKWOODS GA, LOST???"

MARCH 5:

Dear Dennis:

I miss you more each day but we are into our 6 month and it feels like years since I have held you. I feel it should be getting better, but driving through Jax and seeing the hospital where you started your Bio-Med career really hurt. As I crossed the state line I said, "Ok buddy we are home, aren't you glad I brought you along". I know you were with me but seeing our old places without you was more than I could take and I feel that without you, it's not "ours" anymore. This is a part of moving forward, when you know you can't go back. I love you and I am proud to call myself your wife.

MARCH 7:

Dear Dennis:

I think of you today with much pride. Each day brings a memory of something you did for us, for the kids, for me, for our family. I look around and am reminded of all that you brought to this home with love. Sure we had bad days, angry moments and struggles, but in the end we were never without our love for each other. When I spend the moments in silence and open my mind and heart, I know you are there, I can feel you—rest peacefully my love. Always, Debra

MARCH 7:

Dear God:

I am a Mother of an 18 yr. old son who is taking the keys in hand tonight for the first time and driving alone. I have done my part I believe. I tried to set a good example when driving. I was his side kick for some time and pointed out the do's and don'ts of it all. I talked to him last night about NEVER texting and driving. We talked about NEVER drinking and driving, about NEVER taking your eyes off the road to mess with the "tunes". I feel that I have done all that a Mom can do, up to and including praying to YOU that he will return to me safely. He is going to make his first drive to CHURCH so I am hoping since he is coming to see YOU, maybe you will be extra protective today with our boy. I thank you for letting me be the Mother of this special young man and I thank you more for watching over him each time he gets behind the wheel. Love, Tim's Mom.

MARCH 7:

Is it bad when the FISH GUY (cleans the tank) leaves a message that starts with . . . "Hi Debra, I heard Bon Jovi and thought of you . . . ." HA.

MARCH 8:

I have so much "stuff" that I must do. When Dennis was here he handled bills, paper work, sorted the mail and just gave me the "important" stuff to handle—that worked. Now, I don't want to even open the mail as it means "one more thing" I have to do. It's very hard becoming "two" people. If I was a single Mom from the beginning I think it would be different. Becoming a single Mom and running the household by myself "all at once" is a little overwhelming at times. I will figure it out . . . and while I do . . . I will make a list of priorities . . . #1 on list . . . . COFFEE !!!!

MARCH 8:

It is NEVER a bad day when you come home from exercising and your daughter says, "Your butt looks good Mom!" and then your son says, "Yep, it's definitely working (meaning Curves)." Of course I giggled, blushed, gave Tim the keys to the car and Sarah my credit card !!! HA (NO ! BUT I DID GIGGLE AND BLUSH)

MARCH 8:

Anyone who knows country music knows Garth Brooks, and if you made it that far you know his song THE DANCE. Ask me what a WIDOW should NEVER listen too on the way home from town. No ask??? OMGosh . . . . "Holding you, I held everything. For a moment, wasn't I the king. But if I'd only known how the king would fall, then who's to say you know I might have changed it all". "I could've missed the pain, but I'd have had to miss the dance". Ohhhhhhhhhh . . . that's a tear jerker—heart breaker of a song !!

MARCH 9:

Here we go again . . . it is raining, I just stubbed my big toe (ohmyfreakin'Gosh) that hurt, I have the SAME OLE' pinched nerve in my back, and I just heard a song that about sent me into tears . . . BUT I WANT YOU TO KNOW . . . DESPITE ALL OF THAT . . . I am smiling, it is going to be a good day and by Gosh, it's FRIDAY !!!!!

MARCH 9:

Dear Dennis:

See you are STILL taking care of me. My back hurt so bad this morning and as I sat here thinking about how I wish it would stop . . . a light bulb went off. You bought me a chair back massager some time ago and I had it in the closet stored away. (Why? Who knows !). Anyway, I got it out, hooked it up, and it even has a heat setting. I already feel better ! Thanks hon ! That light bulb was you, wasn't it? ♥ Always, Debra

MARCH 10:

Dear Dennis:

I can't even tell you how much I wish you were here. I want to talk to you and tell you about my day and giggle over the silly things. I want to watch a movie and hear you say, "Who is that? What did she play in?" because you never could remember a name ! ha. I keep trying to keep you near as painful as that might be. I hope you know how much I miss you Dennis ♥

MARCH 11:

I haven't really bought anything since Dennis died that wasn't a necessity, so here we go . . . I purchased a Tempur-pedic bed and it arrives tomorrow. It is the adjustable one so I can sit up in bed or elevate my feet. I am hoping this helps my back.

MARCH 12:

This is the day that the Lord made and I AM glad in it. Rain or no rain . . . you can't stop the sunshine in my world today, (at least I hope you can't!) LOL ! Have a great safe, blessed and joy filled day my friends & family.

MARCH 12:

Dear Dennis:

You always said I was stronger than you, which is pretty much a funny thing to those that knew you. You had amazing strength. I use this strength that you saw in me to make it through each and every day. I hate waking up at 3 or 4 a.m. missing you, that hurts, but I am trying to keep the "one day closer" in my mind, and think of all the things I need to do that you will be able to see through me while you are resting way up high. Keep that beautiful smile shining down on us, we love you very much honey !! Always, Debra

MARCH 12:

Just putting it into perspective . . .

When you have lost a loved one as I have, or even a job, promotion, friend, broke up with your significant other, it's so very hard not to be angry and say "why me?". Someone said to me the other day about Dennis, "it's like he was just plucked from the earth". Yes it is. It is very much like that.

When losing someone you love dearly, it may be true that you were not a person of faith before but if you loved that person, you will naturally want to know they are ok. Just as you would when your kids, for example, leave for school. You can't go with them, you must trust and have faith that all is going to be ok until the last bell rings and the bus pulls up at the end of the day.

That faith, of your kids in school, is strong in part because you KNOW where they are. They are at school, on property protected by many adults, rules and even law enforcement in some places. In this example you can actually see "there" (the school), maybe you have been "there" with them before. However, in the case of death . . . we go as we came, alone. Dennis went "there" and I can't go "there" with him.

We don't know where "there" is, we can't go with our loved one to make sure they are ok, we can't say we've "been there" or we "know" there, because until we "get there" we only know what we have been told. So, what do you do? Quit looking? Would you quit looking for your kids if they didn't get off that bus at the end of the day? No, when we can't see and we don't know, sometimes we have no choice but to go on faith.

I have never been a "bible thumper", an overly religious person, was not raised in a church and always felt it was a secret only others knew. As I have said before I get angry with those that talk the talk but don't walk the walk.

God decided it was time and my faith has been tested. "Now (these current days), losing Dennis, 9/25 was the biggest "TEST" of my life" but it did one amazing thing for me . . . it opened my eyes to see ALL of the many "QUIZZES" (if you will) I have taken along the way. My point . . . (I usually have one . . . ha). Some people think that when someone loses someone or has something significantly tragic occur in their lives they FIND GOD. I don't think I "FOUND HIM" I believe HE was there all along. HE wrote the many quizzes that I took. HE was teaching me chapter by chapter, day after day from birth, and when 9/25 came, this just happened to be one of the biggest—"TEST" I was asked to take. Did I pass? I won't know that until I see "there" for myself and step up and ask the teacher for my final grade. Until then . . .

MARCH 13:

I know I talk about Dennis and my faith and God all the time, and just when I think everyone is going to de-friend me for it, I get the nicest, sweetest, private messages. Thank you all so much for letting me use FB to get through this !! I pray you NEVER lose a loved one and have to go through this but if you do, I pray that somehow I will be able to help you get through it as you have me.

MARCH 13:

Dear Dennis:

I put your pictures away for a while. It's just too hard. Constant reminders. Maybe when I am stronger I will bring you back out (ha) don't you love it Dennis how I can put you in a drawer and pull you back out when I need too. Its ok honey you are in my heart & mind so all those Kodak moments are recorded forever ♥ ♥ ♥

MARCH 13:

K I am excited again (are you seeing my ups/downs and calling the therapist yet? lol). Tim and Jake are in Govt. WE just did Chapter 5-Section 1-Outline. I read, we decided what was important and we all did an outline. We discussed, explained, asked questions. Tomorrow night, Section 2 ! By God these boys are going to get a high passing grade if it's the last thing WE do !!! I love Govt. It was my favorite class (thank you Dad for making me watch the news at night) and Thank you to one great teacher for keeping me interested.

MARCH 14:

Dear Dennis:

You always said I was "crazy" but I am sure you meant that lovingly. You did mean that lovingly didn't you? ha. Well anyway . . . This getting over you is a tough tough thing. It would make you crazy I know. You used to get mad when a cold wouldn't go away after 3 days so I can't imagine you dealing with this kind of thing well. No one does. I am up and down still. The down days are few and far between but they are still here. The up days are great. Thank God us GIRLS know how to immediately taken action and hit the stores when we feel it (DOWN) coming on!! Sarah & I have devised a strategic plan that involves Olive Garden, Rue 21, and the Ross store to combat the issue. She says, "I hate when you get depressed, but if it has to happen be sure to bring me along !" LOL (She is so 16 !!!) I miss you sweetheart !!! Always, Debra

MARCH 14:

Apparently the NEWS OF THE DAY is that Marie Osmond had a laughing spell and wet herself on stage. (Nice that they report this kind of crap! Poor lady!) I am curious about something however, I crack up and pee myself daily and not a member of the media has EVER contacted me! NOT ONCE I TELL YOU!

MARCH 14:

I have an announcement !! Shhhhhhhhhhhh . . . everyone listen. I, Debra Jane Blood, purchased a BELT yesterday !! Yep, that's the announcement. If you knew how long it's been since I had a waist and could wear a belt—this would be earth shattering news to you too !!! I found a black dress this weekend at the thrift store, (yes, I shop there.) It was a name brand, fitted, lined and like brand new. The only thing missing was a thin belt (dress already had the loops). I found the belt last night that is white with tiny black polka-dots !! Goes with the dress perfect and fits great. Yay !! It's the little things in life !

MARCH 16:

OK that was NOT a fun Doctors visit. I had what started as a freckle, turn into a mole and then started to change shape, size and color so she removed it for biopsy. It is on my upper left arm. I don't think they will need to amputate just yet, but this was the first time I have had stitches in 16 years and I won't go into detail about the other ones (How old is Sarah?) lol. It didn't hurt while she was doing it but now that the numbness has worn off . . . geesh !!!

MARCH 17:

Dear Dennis:

I went to Lowe's today, by myself, went straight to the plumbing section, found what I needed, measured it against what I had and as I was walking away a young man said, "Can I help you?" I laughed (right out loud), held up my items with much pride and said, "No no you may not I found what I needed and please note BY MYSELF YES-ER-REE BOB (even though I am sure that was not what his name tag said)." You would have been so amazed, stunned and proud of what I can accomplish on my own these days. That does not mean I am happy to do it without you but it's always good to know I can. OK, I was not buying a generator but that was not the point of the story !! LOL Always, Debra

MARCH 17:

You know it's the right decision Dennis, because up there all decisions are made out of love and all love is unconditional !! ♥ ♥ Miss you ♥ ♥

MARCH 18:

Just had a fun "girls out" afternoon. Found an awesome lighthouse (with the light that spins around) run by solar, to sit by the pool. Dennis always wanted one of those so I figured this would be an "authorized purchase".

MARCH 19:

Dear Dennis:

We share and honor your life in our laughter, our tears, our sorrow and our joy !! You gave us so much, taught us so much, and now you guard us and guide us from way up high. You were so unique and special and left such an impact on those that knew you. You were a remarkable man (more than you know) and your time here was just as remarkable and that is why it has been marked with a stamp that says, "Loved deeply, missed truly, remembered forever". Always, Debra

MARCH 19:

GOD LOVE THE ELDERLY: Last night I made country fried steak. I broke one piece in half and gave ½ ea. to Mocha & Molson. Mom was (touchy let's say) about how I "wasted" food on the dogs when it was good food and "I could eat that for lunch tomorrow". Well first there are 4 other big pieces left anyway and she eats like a bird and I mean (humming) and second EVERYDAY she goes into the kitchen and makes herself a SANDWICH. It could be turkey & grape jelly or shoe leather & mayo, I am telling you it does not matter as long as Mona gets her SANDWICH. So, today I walk into the kitchen, there is ole' Mama at the table with her what? SANDWICH. I pulled out the tupperware of the c.f. steak and said, "Hey Ma, remember when you yelled at me last night for feeding the dog????" (Trust me we have had this convo like 80 times). She laughed and said, "Well I just get used to eating sandwiches so I just make one!" I said, "Ok so it's a habit, I get it!" She says, "NO, IT'S NOT A HABIT, sometimes I shake things up !!". FOLKS—I don't know what that (shake things up) means exactly but I am sure there is a new reality TV show on the horizon called "Mona goes wild" Hello Fox TV—we have run out of bread and . . .

MARCH 20:

Dear Dennis:

Well . . . I just miss you, that's all.

Always, Debra

MARCH 21:

Mama Blood is on a roll this week.

ME: Ma we are going to go out to eat tonight if you want to get yourself fixed up a little.

MA: (Who is just outside my door in the hall) OH, save your breath or go talk to my hearing aids, I left them on the kitchen table !!

ME: LOL—OK Maaaaa!!! LOL.

MARCH 22:

Dear Dennis:

You made it all seem so easy—if I took any of that for granted—please forgive me—this being you and me is not what I would call an ENTRY LEVEL position. I love you forever and miss you each second of the day!!! Always, Debra

MARCH 23:

Leaving out the "widow" factor I would just like to say God Bless the "single parent" as it's so very difficult to be all things to all people, make all things happen, keep everyone in line, not miss a thing, and have all the answers. Tired might be a word we could use.

MARCH 24:

Well today I started out puking and it's only gotten better from there. Dr. removed the stitches from where they removed the mole on my arm and she said the Pathologist called her and said he didn't like what she is seeing but is not certain what IT IS and was sending it to CALIFORNIA to another Pathologist to look at it. Oh frickin' goody . . . now I got the fever going and I feel I shall be logging some bed time this weekend. Ask me if I miss Dennis about now?

MARCH 25:

Dear Dennis:

Today is a milestone that I never wanted to mark. Today is 6 months of you in heaven, my heart broken, river of tears fallen, and a billion prayers sent to God to protect and care for your soul. Things have definitely changed with you gone, some good yes, some ok yes, some heart breaking definitely, but change has come none the less, and we can't stop it that is for sure. While I NEVER thought I would spend even 3 weeks without you, I have somehow survived 6 months. This is 6 mos. closer to the time we shall meet again. I love you today as I loved you 6 mos. ago, as I will love you 6 yrs. from now . . . miss you so very much !!! Always, Debra

MARCH 26:

Not really sure what I did to be TESTED so (and I know it's not about ME) but this morning I heard a crashing noise, it was Mom taking out the hutch in the kitchen with her head. She fell and injured her head and arm. (NOT HER HIP THANK GOD). I took her to the ER where we spent 3.? hours getting CT, X-rays, stitches and TLC. She is ok but quite black/blue and sore. While there we got talking to the X-ray tech who (of course) knew my husband, as Dennis fixed the Imaging equipment at this hospital too. She said he was so very loved there and respected and just the other day they were talking about how much they missed him. What made me giggle was she said, "He always knew what to do, and he was so nice and HE KNEW EVERYONES NAME !!" Wait? What? You sure you meant Dennis? He was the one that said in EVERY movie . . . "What is her name?" I love hearing how others thought of him !! You make me proud baby !!! Now that the FUN is over, I am going to TRY to chill, make some coffee and go back to work!! Sweet Jesus . . . does the excitement ever end?

MARCH 27:

Just wondering Dennis . . . if you are really with me . . . could you just pat me on the back with one of your wings please so I know you are here? Ok wait . . . you with wings! That right there is enough to make me giggle. Did you do that? I was just wishing you were here to make it all better and that image alone did the trick! Love you honey.

MARCH 28:

Dear Dennis:

Since you were a BILLS fan and used to say this all the time, I would just like to offer . . . "Now would be a really good time to make a COMEBACK!!"

MARCH 29:

Dear Dennis:

I know I try so very hard to say my prayers each night, and in those prayers I always ask God to tell you how very much I love you still and miss you. If the day is long and difficult and I lay down and sleep comes before my prayers are said, I wonder . . . do you ever ask God, "Did you hear from her today?"

SABBATH, BLACK SABBATH

It's hard to say how we select our "best friend" or our "BFF" (as current terminology dictates), but the one thing we do know is that we select and accept them for good and bad. We do not turn them away when we see their flaws and we do not turn our backs in jealousy when we find that their gifts out match ours 10 to1. If you had a best friend that could scale an 8-foot fence like Superman would you quit being his friend as you were too envious of his skills? What if he stole stuffed animals from small children, had a shoe fetish that no one could really explain, his widely known talent was being strong enough to crush a beer can with one single blow . . . would you still tell the world he was your BFF? What if your best friend was single handedly responsible for causing enough havoc that could send those big beautiful church hats flying into the sky at the end of a Sunday Gospel Revival, would you be too embarrassed to claim him? What if he would leave you for up to three days at a time with no call or word, while you worried and suffered through the endless "what if's? Would you still be there for your friend when he finally returned? Would you still love him unconditionally?

What if, just what if it was true . . . that a dog really was a man's best friend?

His name was Sabbath and he was "the" black lab of all black labs. His owner, master or HBFF (Human Best Friend Forever) was Dennis. Dennis was a huge Black Sabbath (Ozzy) fan so it only seemed right to bestow such a name on the precious pup that he was given as a housewarming gift. They had 16 long years together. He was truly Dennis' best friend, his buddy, his comforter and protector. He stood by his side, slept by his feet, and was there through every up and down Dennis had for years. Life was good for these two. You could say it was nearly perfect, until . . . well until . . . Dennis met Debra.

We had not been together long when I realized that every church in Jacksonville was going to stop at our house at least once to try to bring us to the Lord by way of their church. This happened all the time and most times I simply took the paperwork they provided, thanked them, advised them that I was a Christian and they went on their way.

This particular night the doorbell rang and there was the minister of a local church in which our kids went to the associated daycare. He asked if he could come in and speak to us for a moment about a membership at his church. I admit that I felt somewhat obligated to hear him out due to the kid's enrollment. Dennis had already decided previously after attending a service there that this was not the place for us as he did "not get a good feeling."

Trying to be nice I advised the minister he could in fact come in but only after "I secure the dog", as he was known to be a little protective. It was a football Sunday so when Dennis walked into the front room with a beer in his hand, I am sure I cringed just a little. He grabbed the dog by his collar and began to steer Sabbath to the other room. Sabbath had dug his feet firmly into the carpet to let us know that he was clear on what his job was and that he did not want to leave before he was done showing us his teeth and letting us hear his intimidating low growl. Apparently he had the same "sense" about the minister as Dennis.

When I said, "Sabbath", the minister said with such excitement, "Oh that is so wonderful, you named him Sabbath after the day of rest, that really says a lot about your love for the Lord, and we would love to have others who love the Lord as much as we do to come and share in our service etc. etc. etc." He was talking so rapidly and with such enthusiasm about our choice in a pet name I was certain God was smiling down upon us at that very moment with great pleasure. The minister was still speaking when my husband stopped dead in his tracks with the dog still in tow and said very firmly, "No! Black Sabbath! You know? Ozzy? The best rock band EVER? He's a BLACK lab and his name is SABBATH? Get it?" Looking back I am certain the only thing missing from his sentence was the word "Dude". The minister just stared at us with no expression at all and then said, "Well, uh, no I don't know them, but uh I am sure they are great, however it seems I had that one wrong didn't I?" He handed us some pamphlet on his church, turned and said his good-byes and was quickly on his way.

When I walked into the kitchen still stunned at what was said and the fact that it all took place in a matter of moments, I found Dennis and Sabbath bonding over "yum yums" as we loved to call Sabbath's treats. I gave Dennis that look. You know the one that said, "Really? What was that?" He dismissed me with a smile and without missing a beat patted Sabbath on the head and said, "Good Boy Sabbath! We are not praising the Lord with someone who has such bad taste in music!"

SABBATH—IT'S ME OR YOU DOG

I worked the 4p.m—midnight shift at the time so days were all about me and Sabbath. His small piece of the world was our little back yard on Treemont St. that was surrounded by an 8-foot high fence. Dennis always said that Sabbath "had a knack of getting out" (total understatement) no matter what measures he put in place to put the pup in lockdown.

This particular day I decided I was smarter than the dog and I had just about enough of chasing his cute furry self around the neighborhood while Dennis was at work and trusting me with the care of his BFF. After leaving him out back for what I felt was the appropriate amount of time that would cause him to have a "moment of clarity" about where he really wanted to spend his day, I walked out our back door onto our screened in porch. Alongside the porch was a gate that opened to the sidewalk that ran along the side of the house, onward to the street and the front yard. Sabbath was not onto my clever ways, and had no idea that I was standing there observing what his special doggy Superman abilities were and how they could launch him over an 8-foot fence with ease. To my amazement and amusement I watched as this dog literally backed himself up all the way to the furthest point from the gate that he could get. Without another thought needed in his highly calculated plan he burst forward in a full speed ahead run until he leaped as high as he could which placed his body directly on top of the gate at mid sternum. While it looked incredibly painful to me I watched as he kicked his back feet hard and fast to assist the rest of his body over the top of the fence.

I promise you he was in mid-kick when I did my own "burst full speed ahead" through the door, up the stairs, through the kitchen, pass the dining room, out the front door and rounded the side of the house. It was then and there I heard the screeching sound of doggy brakes. He skidded to a stop with a look of utter doggy disdain. "Oh yes Sabbath, I am on-to-you buddy!" That was "the" day that Sabbath really met the "new girlfriend" and his life had forever changed, and if you would have asked him it was not for the better! From that moment forward it was a battle of wills, a struggle of who was going to outsmart, out run, and outlast the other . . . me or the dog. I am pretty sure, all tallied, it was a tie!

SABBATH—YOUR DOG IS A THIEF

We as humans are collectors by nature. I collect covered bridge items as they take me back to memories of Amish country and the sites of southwest Michigan. It's a common thing amongst us humans, but did you know that we are not the only species that do this? I didn't know at first where they were coming from but it started with one or two and before you knew it I was starting to believe that people thought we were the drop off location for Toys for Tots!! Stuffed animals everywhere. Small, big, new, old, clean, dirty always on our front porch steps. Well being the intelligent people we were it finally occurred to us . . . Ah-ha !! The stuffed animals were showing up on the days that Sabbath was adorning his Superman cape and clearing the fence.

One fine morning as I was relaxing before my afternoon shift, I busied myself with Sabbath by my side. I heard the doorbell ring and with my four-legged, self—appointed body guard walking in step with me, I answered the door. When I opened the door, leaving the screen door closed I saw on the other side a woman on our front steps. What appeared to be her husband in a van was pulled up at the curb directly in front waiting for her. I was sure she was going to hand me a church bulletin, ask me to support her cause, or make a request on behalf of some other charity in need. I was not prepared for what I heard next.

She pointed down to Sabbath who I am certain "grinned" at her and said something "sweet" under his breath. She said in a rather perturbed voice, "Ma'am YOUR DOG needs to be locked up. It has come to my house and repeatedly stolen things from us and I am about tired of it." Well, oh my goodness were you saying my dog was a thief? Not only that, with the tone she used it sounded as if he was already nearing the end of the "three strikes you're out program". That is a very strong accusation to be making both Sabbath and I concurred. I wanted to close the door and consult with Sabbath to see if he could provide any feedback that would clear him of these said "charges" but I didn't feel he would "cooperate with my investigation" as well as I had needed. So, I did what any sane person would do "on the fly" and I denied all charges until I could get proper legal representation and tried to clear Sabbath's name with a lie. I said, "I am sorry if you feel my dog did this, when exactly were your things taken and what was taken?" Apparently she was not happy that I would even question her position so she up'd her game a little and became a bit more forward. She replied, "They were taken from my garage TODAY, they were mine and my husband's shoes and you WILL keep your dog tied up or we WILL have him picked up by the dog warden!" It was then no longer about **if** Sabbath did or did not do this, I was now a protective "Mother" and a little bent out of shape that she was attacking my "child" like this. I mean come on lady, look at that face does it look like he would do anything like you have just described? I said, 'Well Sabbath has been home all day with me, (yes I was his alibi) and I will be sure he remains tied when he is out, and YOU will be sure to CLOSE YOUR GARAGE so NO dog takes your things, thank you and have a great day!" With that I closed the door in the mean lady's face as Sabbath said "thanks for having my back Debbie". She stomped off the porch and was heading to her husband in the van. I was sneaking a peak out of the blinds and had my other hand on Sabbath's head petting him telling him I was pretty sure she had the wrong dog when I see her stop at the curb, bend over and pick up something with both hands. It was then that I realized she was holding two pairs of sandals. One small like a woman's and one large like a man's. "Hmm?" (Came from both Sabbath and I at the same time.) Well how do you like that? GUILTY AS CHARGED !!!

SABBATH—PRAISE THE LORD AND PASS THE HAT

When we lived on Treemont St. in Jacksonville, just around the corner was a southern revival church. On any given Sunday you could see the women coming in and out of this church in the most extravagant beautifully colored dresses and matching hats. It almost seemed there was not a woman in attendance that didn't have a hat on her head.

Dennis and I were relaxing and getting ready to cheer on our Buffalo Bills in a big game and I had let Sabbath out the back while I cooked dinner and prepared for kickoff that would take place in a couple of hours. Dennis opened the back door to check on Sabbath when he realized he had cleared the fence once again and was gone.

We shut off the stove and jumped into Dennis' sturdy black Chevy truck and began driving around the neighborhood looking for our sweet pup that just could not be caged for the love of doggy bones. As we came to the corner where our street intersected with the street that held the address to this church all we saw was 30 to 40 bright colored hats flying in the air, and arms waving. There was color everywhere and everyone seemed to be scurrying about in a panic. We stopped at the stop sign and stared both knowing in our hearts what had caused this ruckus. Flying at a rate of speed that would have been considered record breaking in most sports arenas, here came a cat running out of the hat throwing crowd for dear life and hot on its trail and tail is who . . . yeah, you got it!

Pass the donation plate, yes he's ours!

SABBATH—HE WAS FINE WHEN WE BROUGHT HIM TO YOU

When Sabbath passed we took him to the local animal hospital and Dennis insisted that he be cremated with his remains brought home to us. He was so upset to lose his best friend and for all of the hard times I gave him over this dog, I think I cried harder than anyone. The day we went in to pick up the remains I was certain that Dennis would fall to pieces. Now that I have suffered loss and know how laughter can erupt out of nowhere at the most inopportune moments, I see what was happening to my husband just before we opened the door to walk in and bring our baby home.

I reached for the door and Dennis said, "Wait!" I stopped and turned to him thinking he needed one last moment to gather himself for what was certainly to be considered a sad moment for anyone who has lost a pet. Instead he said with much uncontrolled giggling, "When they hand us the urn that has Sabbath in it, I am going to say to the girl, "WHAT? HE WAS FINE WHEN I BROUGHT HIM TO YOU!" Oh dear God. We had to pull ourselves together from giggling before we went in and I made him promise he would do no such a thing. He did use his line on her but was not quite as dramatic as he was when he first shared it with me. The poor girl looked stunned. I was very quick to reassure her that he was distraught with grief and therefore could not be accountable for his behavior. We brought Sabbath home that night and placed him on the shelf of our dresser. When I said, "How long will we keep him there?" Dennis replied, "He goes when I go Debra." You may just want to read that chapter.

That year I sent Christmas cards with a black lab pup standing at the feet of Santa looking up. I pray that Sabbath and Dennis are walking together side by side as they did in this life, but now on the streets of heaven.

APRIL 2012

(Facebook daily posts)

April showers

APRIL 1:

Getting ready for the summer . . . plants and flowers planted, put out some hanging flowering plants off the deck (purples and pinks—love that), have my little herb garden growing and since 2006 I have been asking my husband for a covered swing for by the pool, well today thanks to an unexpected check due to his hard work and a sale at Wal-Mart—I will be thinking of my honey as I swing soon.

APRIL 1:

It's spring break here in Pickens Co, S.C. so school is out. Therefore, I am praying that I won't be doing an Emergency Room visits, school pick ups, etc. I want to do Curves M-F and Zumba again on Thurs. Might be an aggressive goal but I think I can do it! Sarah told me today I was looking HOT, but then again we were in Wal-Mart and she might have slipped something into the cart just after that.

APRIL 2:

Dear Dennis:

Sometimes I think if the anniversary of your death would just get here and pass it wouldn't hurt so much because "it had been a year" and surely I would be better in a year right? Then I think, somehow I know deep in my heart that in 2 yrs., 5 yrs., 10 yrs. and on the day I die, I will have missed you as much as I do today. I read a blog written by widows the other day. There were women who were married for 40 some years and they sounded just like ME, but it was 3-4 yrs. down the road after they had lost their loved one and they said they still had those WAVES coming in unexpectedly. I guess DEATH knows no time, it doesn't play fair and the pain doesn't care how long you loved, only that you did.

APRIL 3:

Dear God—I know this is your plan, I believe and I shall follow, it is not easy and some days are very hard but I thank you for each breath I take and each sunrise I witness. Today that is all I can do.

APRIL 4:

Dear Dennis:

The ONLY thing that I can think of worse than you being gone . . . is you being gone and forgotten. I will NEVER let that happen. Love you today and always, Debra

APRIL 5:

This is a GOOD NEWS/BAD NEWS POST: Which do you want first? Let's get the BAD news out of the way—THE MOLE!!! It is cancer cells and I have to go to a dermatologist and have more cut out to find out where the "spreading" stops. Isn't that special? Not what I wanted to hear but ok, it's going to be fine.

GOOD news—WEIGH IN / MEASURE UPDATE: Down 3.5 lbs. and 6 more inches !!!! I have lost a total of 13lbs. and 20" inches overall since 12/27. I would like to say more on the pounds but again, the weight doesn't matter as the clothes sizes are getting smaller and smaller. I figure once they cut out the remainder of the mole I should be down a few more ounces for sure SO IT'S ALL GOOD.

APRIL 5:

The will of God will never take you where the Grace of God will not protect you.

APRIL 8: EASTER SUNDAY

HE has risen and I am saved, and we are so loved, in a way that nothing or no one on earth can understand or duplicate. Today I think of you Dennis and the buttered lambs that you always bought to put on the dinner table as it was a memory of Easter's past from your childhood. I think of the FIRST Easter in our new home in Easley S.C. Cosmo the cat caught and decapitated (sorry folks) 3 bunnies and laid them symmetrically on the garage steps for us to find (he has poor timing like me). I think of the meals we made together, the baskets we were so excited to give the kids, the prayers we said for those who celebrated with Jesus in heaven. HE has risen and I am saved, and so were you, so I WILL see you again my love, I will ! ♥

APRIL 9:

Debra walks into the tire repair shop and says all very confident like . . . "You remember when I was in here and you filled my tires with air and that seemed to solve the issue for oohhhh about a minute? Well I am back because the light keeps coming on saying I have low air in the tire, but I stopped and put air in the front LEFT tire as I think that is the one, can you check please?" He takes my phone number and pulls up the account (that was under Dennis' name) and tells me to come back in 40 minutes. I do and as I walk in he says, "Mrs. Bujan . . . ow??, Mrs. Buja.???, Mrs. Bu . . . (I firmly say DEBRA at this point). "Mrs. Debra . . . you know that air you put in the front LEFT tire—well that was over inflated. and by the way you had 3 nails in your back RIGHT tire, but hey you did give it your best shot ma'am !!!" ha. Good God almighty I need a man on standby . . . anyone??

APRIL 10:

Trust in the Lord with all your heart, and lean not on your own understanding. Proverbs 3:5 NKJV

APRIL 10:

Dear Dennis:

You know how we had that deck but never used it. I have it covered with beautiful flowers and the cardinals are loving Gma's birdfeeder. I spoke to some of your family on Easter. I know you would have wanted me to make those calls and keep them close. I still do everything with you in mind, and imagine I always will. I miss you my love.

APRIL 11:

I have never been afraid to say it like it is (no kiddin'?) . . . or never been embarrassed to share how I feel (you got that right?) Well I think I am the happiest—most depressed—loneliest—independent—strong—person I know. I can't begin to tell you what it's like to lose your best friend. The one person you shared every minute with and as sad as it is . . . no amount of activity, no amount of friends, no amount of reading, watching TV, exercising, helping the kids, gardening, or anything can take away this overwhelming sadness I feel with him gone. Will it last forever? No. But does it hurt now . . . OMG yes. I wish I had a time machine.

APRIL 11:

Dear Science:

I would like to donate two teenagers to you now . . . I know this may seem a little bit premature but I feel that they may have faulty wiring that tends to make them argue, disagree, and otherwise ignore all things mature and wise that comes forth from their mother's mouth! With your time and resources there is no doubt that you will be able to find out what makes them tick and stop them from . . . ticking . . . while possibly sparing other parents the torture, I mean concern that I have been going through. No seriously Science . . . . TAKE THEM NOW !!!! Thank you !!! Concerned Mom. (P.S. Is this donation tax deductible by the way? !!! Just curious !)

APRIL 11:

The weatherman said "Frost, bring in those plants people!" I JUST BOUGHT THEM AND PUT THEM OUT FOR CRYING OUT LOUD. So Tim & I carried in 28 plants, hanging flower baskets, herbs, etc. off the deck. I thought this was for ONE night. This morning weatherman says "Maybe two more days" . . . . Ok, my family room looks like a funeral parlor and the cat is out there right now trying to decide which one to potentially use as a litter box and which one to eat, while Gma is saying, "Ohhh isn't that one pretty, and Ohhhhhhhhh that one too, isn't that one pretty, now what is that Deb, I know it's a flower, haha, but what kind of flower???"—"I don't know Ma, I am like YOU and went with Ohhhhhh isn't that one pretty when I bought them!" hahaha. If you look closely on my mailbox it really says . . . 109 Looney Bin Blvd., Crazy town, USA."

APRIL 12:

Dear Dennis:

It's been 7 months soon. 7 long months since the day you left us. I think I have cried 7 billion tears, said 7 trillion prayers, and thought 7 ga-zillion times how I wish you could just walk back through that door and hug me one more time. Tell me you are waiting for me and you are with me each second of the day. While I believe in Jesus and believe in my heart you are with him and with me in spirit, It's that human part of us that doubts, that second guess', that finds it so hard to go on faith when our heart is broke. Isn't it our heart that carriers our faith. So when our heart is broke isn't it harder to hold that faith in, or hold it closer to us? I thought you were the strongest man on earth, I held you up as the smartest person I knew, I loved you because no one was more handsome, more funny or more loving and now I realize that truly it all came down to no one loved me like you did !!!

APRIL 13:

Dear Dennis:

I find it odd that you do not come to me in dreams. You have come to others in this manner I have been told. I must believe it is because you do not see the need to do so because you are already with me each second of each day. I pray that when I get to heaven you will show me all the good, all of the amazing sites as you would have done here on earth. You loved our road trips and you were always filled with wonderment just like a child. I so loved that about you. If you are with me today, please push me along to do the things that I would "rather not do" . . . allow me to move forward and never doubt for one second that I am loving you still with all my heart ! ♥ Debra

APRIL 13:

Dear Dennis: Help me bring Mocha, Shami and Mallard home please. Love you.

APRIL 14:

ANIMAL CONTROL CALLED—THEY JUST PICKED UP ALL 3 OF THE DOGS. THANK YOU GOD and ALL THOSE THAT ASSISTED INCLUDING YOU DJB !

APRIL 14:

Dear Dennis:

I planted the garden today. I thought of you of course. I laughed at the memory of the first garden in South Carolina that you and Tim made for me on that Mother's Day. The next day we spent at the ER because you both had poison ivy. Bless your hearts . . . you sat there like a Panda Bear with a respiratory problem and Tim getting his shots in his pretty little backside while his face looked like someone beat him half to death. OMGosh and I did what any loving Mother/wife would do . . . take pictures and laugh (of course after I knew you were both ok). Tim said, "Those had better be some damn good tomatoes Mom!" lol. I miss you so much today, well that's not really it I miss you so much every day. I know you are with me. Loving you always, Debra

APRIL 15:

Dear Dennis:

You know that hill on the side of our house, just outside our bedroom window? You know, the one that YOU had to cut with the riding lawn mower because it was SO steep that I would NEVER EVER CONSIDER getting on the lawn mower to cut it because I thought it would tip over while I was doing it. You remember you used to say, "What would you do if I wasn't here lady?" and I would say, "Consider it a jungle and buy a couple of swinging monkeys to watch from my window!" Yeh, that one . . . that one I just got on the riding lawn mower and CUT WITHOUT YOU !!! I am here to report that I didn't tip over AND I think I heard you say . . . "HA. Where's the monkeys now Debra?" This falls under . . . "You never know how strong you are until given no other choice". I have to keep setting fear aside . . . no matter how big or small that fear is . . . and go forward. "It is what it is Debra" are your words that I live by. I miss you sweetie !! Always yours . . . Djb♥

APRIL 16:

Dear God in Heaven:

The man you called home that day from our lives is STILL taking care of us from up above. Today I received something in the mail that we would not otherwise have had—had it not been for Dennis. I am so proud of him and so grateful for the man he was and how he provided for his family and loved us. Without a doubt Lord, you have quite an angel in your presence.

APRIL 17:

Tomorrow is the "mole removal". NO not in my yard, on my arm. ha. They said they will cut a piece out (God that sounds like fun), immediately put in under the microscope but it takes 1-1.5 hours to give the results, and if the results are more C Cells they take another, and you know rinse, wash, repeat. So I could be there until A/They get tired and want to go home B/They discover on the first try that I was never a size C in anything or C/ They dig so deep my arm falls off and they figure. "what's the point". I will let you know how that all goes. Thank you to Miss Kristi for driving me "in case I need sedation" (no folks that was right out of the pamphlet they sent me.) HA. It's sounding like a good time will be had by all hey?

APRIL 17:

If you ever lose someone (pet or human) that you love and want some cheap therapy . . . write write write. I have been writing up a storm and wow are the memories flooding back. I will admit I have cried enough tears to fill Lake MICHIGAN up twice but it's so nice to remember when. I know I can't be the only woman who thought she was so in love with her husband that she has chosen to grieve in this manner, however I hope that someday, someday when I am with him again, my words will live on and help another walk through this big black hole they call death. I miss you Dennis—oh how I miss you.

APRIL 17:

Dear Dennis:

I wore your shirt today, I drove your truck, I said your name in prayer and wished for this to be a really long bad dream. God said that wasn't the case so I lay down tonight in our bed, with your shirt on me and dream of better times when we were together and happy and thought "forever" was longer than 16 years. Missing you. Debra

APRIL 18:

Gray hair is a crown of splendor; it is attained by a righteous life. Proverbs 16:31. Well, at least SOMEONE besides L'Oreal gets it.

APRIL 18:

Dear Dennis:

This is one of those days I know you would have taken off work and gone with me. Now as it turns out this is one of those days that I am left to "believe" you are with me anyway. I am using you for strength today sweetie. I love you. Debra

APRIL 18:

Well after "Dr. OMGYOUAREGORGEOUS" got done speaking and rubbing my arm, no more sedation was needed. He was beautiful and funny and sweet and the first words out of his mouth as he held my hand and rubbed my arm . . . "First, you DON'T

have cancer !! . . . Second, SOMEONE should have told you that a long time ago."
He said it was a mole of a certain type and left untreated it would definitely become
an issue but at this point it was not. So he still had to remove layers and test them
and he only had to go 1 layer deep which did leave a HOLE about the size of a
quarter in my arm. They promise it will heal on its own but for now it looks a little
"Ewwww". About an hour after it was over the numbness wore off and ohmymy . . .
that was not cool. Thank you again to my friend Kristi for taking me and staying with
me and brightening what could have otherwise been a nerve-racking day. Thank you
for all of the prayers today friends . . . you pulled me through. Dennis if you were with
me . . . yes I was smiling at that handsome man but if you paid attention we were
talking about the Roswell Cancer Center of Buffalo, NY and how hard it was to be a
Bills fan !!! ha. I am heading to bed early . . . worn out.

APRIL 19:

Good Morning friends . . . It appears when I drink water it shoots out the hole in
my arm! I have sprung a leak! OK that was just a joke. Surprisingly enough while it
hurts it does not hurt quite as bad as I had expected this morning. Thank Goodness.
Running Ma to get a hearing aid check today as when she sleeps she puts her aids
in her SHOES, (the right hearing aid in the right foot shoe, the left hearing aid in the
left foot shoe) I don't know . . . maybe she thinks she can hear herself coming down
the hall! Anywho . . . her transmitter is broke—now Mona Jane SWEARS it's not but
it is and I think she put her shoe on before she put her hearing aid in her ear !!! She
says I am crazy (imagine that) . . . she may be right as Lord knows I have enough
reasons to be! lol

APRIL 19:

Dear Dennis:

I always knew if I had to live without you, I could. I have never doubted my strength
and I believe that was one of the reasons you were drawn to me in the first place.
However, I always knew if I had to live without you, I wouldn't want to. Day after day
goes by and while I am sure I am getting stronger, my heart just breaks each time I
think of you. It is true there are days I don't feel better because it's been longer, I don't
feel better because you are in heaven, I don't feel better or consoled because you
are in peace. That may sound bad but that is the full blown human-truth-selfish-side
of things. I want you home, I want you with me, with us, here, so we can see you,
touch you, talk to you and hold you. So God will have to forgive me as this is what
us humans do when we miss someone. We hear the words said, we believe in the
goodness of God and where your soul resides, but the human side of us wants what
it wants and that is you home . . . with us. Always, Debra

APRIL 20:

Dear Dennis:

This is one of those days that waking up without you is harder than others. I don't know why some days are like this. When someone you are close to passes away you are very aware of how precious this life is and how it can be over in a blink of an eye. I don't say that to be depressing but each minute counts way more than it used too. I miss you my love very much! Always, Debra

APRIL 20:

Ask me what made me cry TODAY? My son's cap and gown arrived. You have no idea.

APRIL 22:

I just came home from Wal-Mart with only a few bags after being gone 2 hours. I was just in one of those get out and wander around and look at everything moods. Sarah said, "OK, where else did you go? Who did you see? Is there a boyfriend that you haven't told me about because you are not sure if I will approve?" LOL OMG . . . Yeh Sarah that's it . . . . I found him in the frozen foods section of the local Wal-Mart !!!

APRIL 23:

Dear Dennis:

I thought of you yesterday and laughed. Want to know why (or should we just go with it's better than crying?). Because I ATE A RASPBERRY JELLY FILLED GLAZED DONUT and I remember when you and I were on vacation in N.C. and before I left I said, "Now don't let me eat tons of bad/fattening food while we are gone". Then while there we stopped at this bakery for a cup of coffee and as I went to put the RASPBERRY JELLY FILLED GLAZED DONUT to my lips you SNATCHED it from my hand, took a big bite and yelled, "SAVED !!! WHAT? I SAVED YOUR HIPS JUST IN THE NICK OF TIME—JUST LIKE YOU ASKED ME TOO !!!". What a great husband you were !!! ha. Miss you SO much my love! Always, Debra

APRIL 23:

There was this apartment complex that was on the edge of the river that ran through Jacksonville. They had this beautiful clear piece of land with a hill that ultimately ran down to the water's edge. You used to take me there just as the sun was going down and we would sit on that hill, watch the sun dance off the water and talk of what our life would be like together . . . "someday". Those were the moments that made me fall in love with you . . . those were the moments that made "someday" possible.

APRIL 23:

OK NOBODY IS GOING TO BELIEVE THIS BUT . . . There is already a "DEAR DENNIS" book and IT IS ABOUT A WIDOW writing to her dead husband to deal with her grief. Who knew? OMGosh. That's ok . . . I have other stories to tell along with my Dear Dennis posts, and I can rename my book easily . . . but WOW !!!! I found it on Amazon.com.

APRIL 24:

Ever have one of those days when you know that previously you have made progress but now you feel like you are drifting backwards? It's an awful feeling. It's not just about Dennis (of course that is part of it), it's the exercise, the confidence, the progress forward with everything. Sometimes it feels "stalled" and I can't seem to push through it and get my momentum back so easily. I wonder about people that live day to day and never question "pushing forward" and never question if "there is more to life than this". I guess as long as you believe you can move forward and you at least have the willingness to do so, even if you can't on any given day, you are actually succeeding with the plan God has laid out in front of you. Just had to think that through. I do my best thinking in written form! ha.

APRIL 24:

I have had more than one friend express "worry" to me lately. Consider this . . .

People gather bundles of sticks to build bridges they never cross. ~Author Unknown"

APRIL 25:

When I discovered that the "Dear Dennis" concept and title was taken, I did not give up, but instead I went in search. I read about selecting a title and what it takes to "grab the reader's attention", make your book "stand out" in a long list of many. Sub-titles are important as well but it's the main title that begs the question . . . "Will you read me? "I have settled on a title and my hope is to have the contents of this book done and ready to publish no later than March 2013. As long as no other widow loses her husband and feels the need to be funny about it between now and then my book will be titled: ***My husband has died, but that's not the funny part.***

APRIL 26:

Ok this may sound silly to you but I miss making coffee for my husband in the morning. I think it was more about bringing him a cup and getting a hug in return with a "thank you Debbie Dear."

APRIL 27:

OMG I bought Mom a birdbath of sorts but I filled it with birdseed and put it on the deck in direct view of where she sits in her chair and looks out. I brought it in due to the rain. She just walked back to my office to say, "Deb can you put the bird feeder back out because it's getting about that time that they will be coming and they are going to wonder where their food is!" Well we wouldn't want that Ma !!!! She is so funny.

APRIL 30:

SAD snuck in today and took over. I hate when that happens and I can't stop it. It's like fighting an enemy you can't see . . . thank goodness it doesn't come around as much as it used too.

7LBS OF SAUSAGE

It is because America is a "melting pot" as they say. We all come from "somewhere" right? Dennis James Bujanowski. Now with love in my heart, I ask you, where do you think his family came from? Yes, of course Poland. He was just a few generations from those that actually came to the United States to make a better life for their family. I loved being married to a man of this ethnicity. Ok, yes some of the jokes are funny and he told most of them himself . . . but you know what? The food was way better.

Some of it is "Polish" food and some of it is native to his hometown of Buffalo, N.Y. but all of it was "Dennis' favorites". There is pierogi. The written definition is dumplings of unleavened dough—first boiled, and then they are fried usually in butter with onion. They are traditionally stuffed with farmer's cheese, sauerkraut, mushrooms, or mash potatoes. My definition is FABULOUS! Pierogis were to be the "key to my success", the "window of opportunity". Yes these little "dumplins" were what I was going to use to get my "dumplin's heart". He said making Pierogis from scratch was what I needed to know how to do to even think about walking down the aisle.

Then we have golumpki (stuffed cabbage), Sahlen's hot dogs, Duck Blood soup—Ok, no I did not try it and would not even think of trying it even though my last name was "BLOOD", my dog was named "MALLARD" because my "POLISH" husband loved "DUCKS". But no—thank you for asking. There is Weber's mustard, Mighty Taco; "beef bean and cheese burrito with sour cream and jalapeno" was what we sang as we crossed the New York State line on each trip to Buffalo. There was Anchor Bar Hot Sauce, and much more to delight the pallet.

Dennis was born and raised in Buffalo (Clarence) N.Y. He was definitely a man who loved what that really meant and loved his food. Chicken Wings were a staple at our house (And I swear to all things Buffalo it was his last meal). But the reason I bring this all up is because of one of his all-time favorite "Buffalo" foods was Holiday Polish Sausage!

Now I am not a girl who likes sausage unless it's kielbasa, but Dennis loved it all. He loved Italian sausage patties as they used them at one of his favorite Buffalo pizza stops on the "Royal Sub." He loved hot Italian sausage links on the grill. But the one that stood out above the rest was "Holiday Polish Sausage". Whenever we made a trip north we always had to stop at the deli before leaving town to get many of his favorites but during the winter months he was on the hunt for his "Holiday Polish Sausage." Dennis brought a cooler with us always, he loaded it with ice and then he packed it full of meats, cheeses and goodies to bring back to our home in Florida or South Carolina.

One particular year we stopped at the deli and purchased 7 lbs. of Holiday Polish Sausage. He was so excited. He had selected it piece by piece and pulled the deli clerk through his tale of "sausage love" as he did. He packed it on ice right there in the grocery store parking lot. He treated it as if it were a heart transplant and we needed to be ever so careful to make sure nothing happened to it before we arrived back home to the recipient (which was him of course). I don't recall praying over it for its safety on the ride home, but had he thought of it . . . *"Dear Heavenly Father of all things sausage . . ."*

These 7 lbs. of sausage weighed heavily (7 pounds heavy to be exact) on his mind. He could barely take the right exits for his brain could not ignore that this mouth-watering delicacy was in the cooler in the back of the truck, just a few feet from where he was perched. He talked about how good it was going to be and how one must first boil it and then grill it and then . . . oh my Lord . . . I relived the entire process and the memories of "sausages past" every 100 miles until we finally made it back home. (Thank you Jesus!)

The very next day he made a plan. He told our friends who lived five houses down the road of the splendid and delightful sausage. He invited them to be a part of what had now become some sort of sacred meal that only special people of his choosing could partake.

He set about his way that day. He had selected the right stockpot, he had put in just the right amount of water and he had made certain the temperature was just so. I was not feeling well that day but then again I was also not as motivated and enthused about the "sacred sausage" event as my sweet husband. I laid down for a nap that afternoon with our black lab Sabbath, Dennis' oldest and best friend at my feet. As I drifted off into my slumber I could hear Dennis' sounds of joy as he prepared and cooked and talked (to himself I am assuming) of how great this was going to be and "Debra I just don't understand you not liking this sausage, it is the best!"

It was hours later when I was jolted awake by my husband SCREAMING from the kitchen. *"Debra, did you eat the Holiday Polish (Sacred) Sausage that I drove all the way to Buffalo, N.Y. for 18 hours in a truck with a cooler that I had packed with ice which I brought especially to carry the Holiday Polish *Sacred* Sausage in?" "Did you?"*

Ok I had just opened my eyes . . . you know how that is . . . that is what I heard but I am sure if witnessed it was more like *"OH MY GOD Debra, did you eat the damn sausage . . . it's gone?"*

Well, I wiped my eyes of the angel dust that had coated them. I shook my head to clear the cobwebs made of silk that I had formed while I slumbered (remember I was slumbering?). I thought for 2.5 seconds before forming what I thought was a very intelligent response of, *"No I didn't eat the Holiday Polish (Sacred) Sausage that WE drove all the way to Buffalo, N.Y. for 18 hours in a truck with a cooler that YOU had packed with ice which YOU brought especially to carry the Holiday Polish *Sacred* Sausage in . . . . dear !!"*

Ok, again, that is what I heard myself say, but I am sure it was more like, *"Hell No, because FIRST you know I don't even like sausage you Pollock (I am so sure I said that lovingly at the time) and SECOND stop screaming at me please because I JUST WOKE UP!!"*

It only took 2.5 additional seconds from there to understand what had happened to the 7lbs of sausage. I hear loud grumpy muttering, *"I (bleepin) boiled it, then I (bleepin) grilled it, laid it on the (bleepin) platter, pushed it to the back of the (bleepin) counter and ran down to the neighbors to tell them that dinner would be at (bleepin) 6 p.m. I was gone maybe, MAYBE 10 (BLEEPIN) minutes and when I got back the platter was (bleepin) empty and . . . ."* (Now if you knew Dennis personally you would understand that generally speaking he was NOT a cussin' man (ha) so I want you to know he was actually saying the word "bleepin".)

It was at this point that Sabbath nor I were slumbering peacefully any longer and we looked deep into each other's eyes. He had this big belly protruding from his side and he was still licking his lips. The look on his face said it all . . . *"Yes I BLEEPIN' DID IT!!! DO SOMETHING ABOUT IT!!!"* Oh dear God, I jumped up, grabbed that "oldest and best friend" by the collar and ran like the wind for the door. I had been accused of trying to kill off Sabbath many times previous to this glorious moment in time but I want you to know on this particular day I was all about ensuring he lived to see another!

Sabbath remained an "outside" dog for about 3 days after this feast. (Great idea there Debbie!) He later confessed completely to the crime and said, he too thought that Holiday Polish Sausage was sacred, was certain that his master had cooked it just for him, he didn't understand my indifference towards the scrumptious meal and swore it was the best he ever had. He explained while getting to the platter on the back of the counter was a little tricky without thumbs, it was well worth it. I tried to tell him that running away was probably in his best interest at that time, but as always he never really listened to me. Remember how I said I had been (wrongfully) accused of trying to "do him in" previously? I am almost positive he was hoping that I would be the "fall guy" on this one. Sorry Sabbath, for this I could not accommodate buddy!

That was 2001 in Florida. When Sabbath passed away in South Carolina in 2006, Dennis said, "I loved that dog so much, but I still can't believe he ate my BLEEPIN' 7lbs of Sausage!" (Let it go honey!)

MAY 2012

(Facebook daily posts)

Come what may

MAY 1:

I told God yesterday that I was sorry I had not been in touch lately and I believe I heard him say . . . "that's ok, I was with you anyway."

MAY 2:

I was told that I looked like I was losing weight by someone who I don't cook for, I am not related too, is not my friend on FB, they don't want to date either of my kids, OR me. LOL OMGosh I think they meant it.

MAY 2:

Dear Dennis:

Remember how you would drive everywhere and I would crochet or read my Kindle because your driving made me quite. oh what is the word . . . jittery? Well now I have to drive everywhere and I am really starting to miss my "CRAFTING WITH DEBBIE ON THE ROAD" as you loved to call it.

MAY 3:

The guest bathroom is starting to rise up from the rubble so to speak. The nasty carpet is gone and there is new pretty tile. The walls have been stripped of the 1970's wallpaper and replaced with a sea-foam bluish/green. The popcorn ceiling no longer pops (ha) it is now scraped, sanded and painted. Tomorrow (hopefully) I will be able to put this beige glaze over the aqua and do some rag-rolling type finish. I already have the shower curtain, rugs, shelves, pictures, towels, etc. to match. It's going to be so cute. Joel "the fish" guy is also Mr. Super Handyman. I am so excited.

MAY 3:

Dear Dennis:

Life sure has a way of moving on whether you want it to or not. Things are changing, the house is changing, Tim will be graduated in nearly a month, Sarah will be heading towards her senior year, and I, well I miss you each and every day while I try to find new things to try, new ways to explore the world and new ideas to stop my broken heart from hurting. I look out over our property and can picture us standing in that same spot when we moved in and how happy and excited we were to call this home. I pray you are resting easy and there is nothing but joy in your soul. Always yours, Debra

MAY 4:

I had to get on FB one last time tonight just to post this . . . I was watching "The three faces of Eve" and for those not familiar this is a 1957 movie starring Joann Woodward. So in this movie Eve (1 of the 3) is out partying, dancing, singing, etc. This guy in uniform tries to "take her home" after she is done singing. She blows him off and he says . . . (PARAPHRASING) . . . ." You are going with me right? I mean after ALL OF THE MONEY I poured into you tonight? Let me tell you what, WHEN I SPEND * * *$8.00* * * ON A WOMAN I EXPECT TO WAKE UP TO MORE THAN THE MORNING PAPER DELIVERED !!!!!!" I am SO sure I shot coffee through my nose laughing. Easy there big spender! K GUYS . . . I need you to put on your math hats here and tell me please . . ."1957 x $8 = 2012 x?"

MAY 4:

Ok I had a thought (and no Mona it didn't hurt) I was noticing all of those LOL's out there and I think that women of our YOUNG age should be using PYM instead of LOL. Are you with me? P=Pee, Y=Yourself, M-Moment. Now doesn't that just make good sense?

May 5:

I woke up wondering what God has in store for me over the next year. There was apprehension, a little anxiety, much excitement but no fear, so that is a good thing. I keep doing one day at a time. I miss Dennis no less today than I did 9/25 but the pain is lessoning I will admit. I hate that EVERYTHING reminds me of him, as sometimes you want to shut that part of your brain OFF so you don't have to remember. I will put my faith in the Lord, and let him lead me where HE will.

MAY 5:

Dear Dennis:

As I painted the bathroom today my mind drifted back to Treemont St. where I must have painted each wall ten times over. You remember all of the colors I went through in our bedroom until I finally got just the "right" shade. After a billion trips to the paint store I finally called you in to give your "approval" of the final product. When I said, "What do you think?" You proceeded with such "caution" and said, "Oh no no, what does Debbie think? Now that's the important question here." Then I come forward to our SC home. You chose this unbelievable shade of green to paint the deck. We argued, we went back and forth, I said it was ugly you said it was "deck worthy". Then you had some man come out to work on something for us and while there you said to him very non-chalantly . . . "Hey man, what do you think of that color green that I painted the deck with?" He tilted his head back and forth like Mocha does when you ask her if she wants to go "outdoors", took off his hat, rubbed his forehead, shifted from foot to foot and finally said, "Ummm . . . It CLASHES WITH THE OUTDOORS !!!!" Of course I spent the next 3 days and a trip to Lowe's to get new paint telling you how "God made the OUTDOORS with 800 gazillion shades of green" and "ONLY YOU would pick the shade of green that would clash with it !". lol. Ahhhh the fun we had with that one. Every time the subject of "painting the deck" came back up you would get that grin and look and say ever so lovingly "Shut up Debra!" LOL. I miss you honey . . . you made life so fun! Always, Debra

MAY 6:

I got on my scale and it said that I lost 100 lbs. !!!!! Soooooo I went and got a new battery and then it told the truth . . . so yes, of course I did . . . I put the old battery back in!

MAY 7:

Dear Dennis:

It seems to me no matter how many years pass, no matter how many miles, whether I find love again or not, I will wake each day that I have left on this earth and think of you, for this I am certain. Some people play a role in your life, some people are a big part of your life, some are your life. You were mine. This month marks 9 years of marriage and at the same time 8 months of you gone. If it is possible to miss you any more than this I wouldn't know how that could be. Always, Debra

MAY 7:

I am way beyond caring if anyone thinks I am crazy, that ship has sailed !! I have had a horrible day. It is a day filled with tears, tons of tears, I want my husband home and I am angry and sad and miss my best friend and I don't give a damn who knows. So I was sitting here crying my eyes out AGAIN and getting sick of crying my eyes out AGAIN and Tim comes in and rubs my back and says, "I am sorry Mom, I love you and maybe Dennis will come to you in a dream tonight." WELL SON . . . not really but close . . . I go into my room and check my cell voicemail. It's Dennis' sweet cousin leaving me a message to tell me she HAD A DREAM LAST NIGHT OF DENNIS. She said he was vibrant, healthy, very happy and just looked wonderful. He made a joke and told her that "they have corrected a few disconnects in his brain and he is good now". Ha ! He told her that he loved me and was really always with me. He said he was with Sarah too and that was his girl. He hugged his cousin in his dream and told her he was really ok now. I guess God heard me today as I don't know how else that could have played out that way. Thanks for letting me share.

MAY 8:

I am so very blessed to have each of you in my life !!! No matter how many times you hear me complain, no matter how many tears, or missing Dennis posts or stories, you keep right on hanging in there with me. You keep lifting me right back up when you know tomorrow I will fall again. I love you for that and I pray that I am to you in a friend what you have all been to me these past 8 months. Today was better and yes, that dream helped for sure. A man that is on my friend's list that I have never met but adore, said yesterday, "We need to share what God does for us, it gives hope to the hopeless". Oh how true those words are . . . Thank you friends—you are the best .

MAY 9:

Dear Dennis:

It's raining today here . . . I am sure it's not doing that up there, you must have sunshine 24/7 you lucky man. So, a funny thing happened on the way to get the mail the other day . . . I was driving your truck, because Tim was driving my car, because the Jeep brakes went out. (because that is the kind of TEST we have been under since you've been gone) and I stopped at the mailbox to get the mail, and after I did and started to pull away I forgot that I was in a vehicle that is like the size of two put together. So if you happen to look down and see green paint on the side of your black truck, just remember . . . the vocabulary up there is limited to all GOOD words . . . So I suspect you will say something like, "Gosh Golly there Sweet Pea did you bump into the mailbox with my truck? Well that's ok Sugar Plum because you were only trying your best !!!" hahahahahaha. Ok, ok . . . . I heard the thunder a few minutes ago . . . I know you were stompin' because God said, "Be nice now Dennis, I am listening!" Loving you . . . Debra

MAY 10:

Dear Dennis:

You remember when I told you the highlight of my life was being the Mom of TEENAGERS? OK, STOP LYING . . . NO you don't because I never said that! HA !! Teenagers just may be the death of me. Timothy needs to be somewhere by 6 a.m. but he is at the house looking for the car keys at 6:32 a.m. Hmmmmm . . . I think he may just be a little, oh shall we say . . . "Tardy". Sarah who gets up 10 minutes before she has to be ANYWHERE, but then does the standard 4 x change of clothes because, "OMG I am not wearing that are you kidding me?" God Forbid the Bus Driver see her in anything less than Prada on a Thursday!

I have spent my Mothering days uttering Mothering ways of how not to be late . . . "Too be early is to be on time" . . . . "Lack of planning on your part does not constitute an emergency on mine?" . . . "the early freakin' bird gets the early freakin' worm" . . . you know all of those smart intellectual things you share with your kids while they are tearing apart the house looking for the keys that they swear YOU had last but THEY left on the kitchen counter, or the closet for the shirt that they argued with you about because "Please Mom I know it's expensive but everyone has one" . . . but now for some reason they wouldn't be seen dead in it !!! OH LORD HELP ME . . . . So, here's the deal Dennis, I know you might only be up to the "make lights flicker and doors slam" class but you could kick her bed a few times and get her moving and you have the best view to locate things better than a rescue dog in an orange vest. So, babe help a "Mother" (sister) out around here every now and then please? K—Love you always, Debra

MAY 11:

Dear Dennis:

As I redecorated the bathroom I had removed the double light switch plate and then put it down and for the love of God I can't find it now. WELL I told Cody to go to the basement to that drawer that you had 800 of these special things saved. He came back with "the only double switch plate" he could find. This one is SPECIAL. How could a switch plate be special you ask? It was covered in thick wallpaper by YOUR MOTHER from wallpaper in her house years ago, and you always saved it. It now hangs in our bathroom and looks like IT WAS MEANT TO BE !!! So, how about that?

A little piece of your Mom is still with us too. I thought you would love that. Missing you today and always, until I hold you again. Debra

MAY 11:

Tim came in my room the other night to ask me where something was (keys, $$, I don't know) . . . Apparently I was WAY SOUND ASLEEP and when I started to speak I said, (quote) "the purple giraffe is over there". He died laughing at me and said something like "No Mom I need . . . .?" I said, "Good luck WITH YOUR QUEST!". Then I got up, went to the top of the stairs and SCREAMED at him for being awake! Yep, that's what happens when you mess with a Mama who has had no sleep in days. Be afraid children. Be very afraid.

MAY 12:

Heavenly Father:

Thank you for this day, for bringing me good friends, great family and wonderful memories of love and better days. Thank you for the tomorrow that is not promised but cherished. Make me stronger and wiser in all I do and become. Amen

MAY 12:

Dear Dennis:

Tomorrow is Mother's day. I remember so many of them that were extra special because of YOU. You always took the kids to get me something, always made dinner special and you never missed a year without making me feel appreciated for being a Mom. This year you will have an extra special one as you will be with your own Mother again. I know how very much you loved her and she you. I miss you honey and think of you every day! Yours always, Debra

MAY 14:

Dear Dennis:

I drive down the road listening to the music . . . hearing these words . . . "the struggles make us stronger, the changes make us wise, happiness has its own way of taking it's sweet time . . . Life ain't always beautiful, tears will fall sometimes . . . Life ain't always beautiful . . . but it's a beautiful ride." Jesus only knows I could not miss you more. I still can't believe you are not here and won't be coming back . . . some days it seems impossible for my heart and mind to accept others I am so very aware that it almost kills me. I still pray for your soul each night and will continue to do so if I live here without you another 50 years. Always, Debra

MAY 15:

Dear Dennis:

You are lucky that you don't get Facebook in heaven, then again you never liked it here so I doubt you would sign up, (though ignoring a friend request from Jesus might not look so good you know what I am saying !?) If this were anything other than you dying you would be saying "Debra, it is what it is, suck it up and get over it" But it's not that easy hon. I wonder if you had to end everyday feeling like this . . . would you still keep the faith and smile? No I am sure by now you would be in jail for a little "road rage" or something "Dennis Like". Remember when I used to cry every time I said good-bye to the kids? You used to throw me in the truck and take me out to eat because your theory was I wouldn't cry in public. Well you were right, but that back fired on ya' didn't it, as in the end you got a smiling 200 lb. wife!. I guess it's true opposites attract, as instead of flipping the bird and "Earnhardt-ing" people on I-95, I choose to exercise and write. A little less risky yes but it eases the pain.

Every time I say or do something crazy Sarah says, "If Dennis heard you . . ." or "If Dennis saw that . . ." and my response is always the same . . . "Well then . . . Dennis shouldn't have died on me and he would have something to say about it !" That may not sound nice, but it's true . . . Every decision is mine now and while I think WWDD *(ha), in the end it's back to "What is Debra going to do?" I miss you . . . well we all get that . . . but I do . . . and the reasons why are just too many to count! Always, Debra

MAY 16:

Tomorrow is 5/17. 9 yrs. Dennis and I would have been married. While it may not make sense to you, I won't be posting tomorrow. It hurts just a little too much to think about all day. I will bury myself in work and then exercise and try to get past this hurdle. Thanks for your understanding and support.

MAY 17: DENNIS AND MY 9TH WEDDING ANNIVERSARY—NO POSTS WRITTEN

MAY 18:

Dear Dennis:

Yesterday was hard. Thinking of you, our wedding, the song that played, you speaking and telling me how much I meant to you during our vows. It all came back and it brought with it many tears. I know that the time we shared was not always easy, and we didn't always handle everything perfect, but I always knew at the end of the day we were right where we wanted to be . . . with each other. I wish to stop marking time now that you are gone. I pray that you were with me somehow yesterday and know that I was so very proud to be your wife. Always, Debra

MAY 18:

Dear friends:

Thank you for all of the messages, love and support yesterday. It was not easy and I wish we could just wipe the calendar clean so we didn't have to get over these kind of hurdles when we lose someone. I worked, I ate dinner and then I went to bed and stayed there. Today is a new day and I will go on with him in my heart and you all by my side. Thank you again . . . losing Dennis has been the most difficult thing I have had to endure but each of you have made it just a little easier to handle. Love you all.

MAY 18:

Dear Facebook:

Since I am your "Queen" I have placed a bid to buy shares of your stock. That is if you don't hit the open market at $5000 a share !! Please be kind as I have been to you all of these years !!!"

MAY 19:

Dear Dennis:

Today our little girl is going to her Jr. Prom. She is going to be stunning and I just wish you were here to see this. I know you are going to be with Sarah today, watching over her, being amazed at what a beautiful young lady she has turned out to be. That silly girl played songs over breakfast and of course one of them made me cry. But then what doesn't do that right? We love you and carry you with us through each amazing new memory made. Always, Debra

MAY 21:

Dear Dennis:

Good Morning my love. We have made it through another milestone and what an event it was. I know you saw Sarah shine all the way up there . . . she was simply stunning. Now as I close that chapter I move towards Tim's graduation. This one is going to be a little bit harder for me without you as we put so much into getting him to this day. I know you are proud of the man he is becoming and I truly believe you will be with us as he walks that stage in June. WE each miss you every day and tears still fall from time to time, but we are getting stronger. I don't feel I am growing away from you anymore, instead closer to the day we see each other again. (Don't get excited it won't be anytime soon!) I will continue to pray for your soul if you continue to watch over us—deal babe? Always, Debra

MAY 22:

The devil doesn't know what to do with somebody who just won't give up.

(Joyce Meyer).

This is true . . . We have all seen the Devil on some level in our lives, I know I have. I refused to give up, to turn my back on Christ, and to let the Devil use his wise ways to take me over. I didn't give up and I am stronger and more blessed today because of it.

MAY 22:

Dear Dennis:

You were amazing in how you provided for your family. God is good and I could not be more grateful for either one of you.

MAY 23:

God wants us to have a present expectation of something good happening to us instead of constantly mourning over what has been lost.—(Joyce Meyer)

Is she talking to me? I don't think TIME heals all wounds, I think GOD heals all broken hearts. I can see the sunrise of tomorrow, the pain is easing, waves still come but I will meet Dennis again and I know that GOD put us together for a reason. While I still mourn and tears still fall, I chose very early on to celebrate his life and to celebrate all that was Dennis, all that was Dennis & Debra, all that was "our love" by posting on here and writing my book. Out of that came "a present expectation of something good happening" and slowly the "constantly mourning" turned into "sometimes", then "less than yesterday", and now "not as much as a few months back". GOD heals all broken hearts, time is just what he uses to allow us the ability absorb what is happening.

MAY 24:

Dear Dennis:

As I prepare for the next few weeks and Tim's graduation I keep you so very close. You may not know but you are a part of all we do, and you are thought of many many times throughout each day. We miss you and it hurts that you are not here with us for this day. It is however through my faith that I know you really are with me each minute of each day and it is through all of the love you gave that Tim knows how very proud of him you are even now. Guide us baby and feel the love that we are sending up to you with each prayer and thought !!! Always, Debra

MAY 25:

You don't have to hang on to anger. You may feel it, but you don't have to keep it. (My girl Joyce Meyer) Well to some this is "easier said than done". I watched anger cut years off of Dennis' life (and it's ok that I say that out loud) bless his heart. I have watched it hurt the kids, friends, family etc. You can hang on to it and think you are going to beat it, come out on top, but in the end, it will weaken your strength, ruin relationships, interfere with careers, scar children and harm those that you claim to love the most. If we could only all "let go and let God" and truly do what is said, "own it, feel it, scream, yell, cry, cuss, and be mad as hell" but THEN give it to God. Once you do it's no longer yours and you did all that you will ever be able to do with it. HE knows what to do and look how FREE you've become by letting it go. I have seen it do some serious damage to many and that is why I "choose" to forgive and to let things go more times than not. I want to live free.

MAY 26:

Ok, there was this really cute man behind me in line at Kmart and I was buying one of those ridiculously huge graduation cards for Tim. He just goes, "Huh . . . couldn't find one bigger?" I thought OMG a smarta$$ after my own heart. I said just as serious . . . "Nope, they only had the little ones!" We both laughed. Then as I was starting to put my stuff in the cart I guess he thought it was his turn and he lifts his card up like he is going to get ready to swipe it. I had not paid for my stuff at that point, so I see this and I said, "Go Ahead, NO REALLY SIR pay for my stuff and you and I will be new best friends!" He said, "I sure wouldn't mind being your friend but I got my stuff eyed at about 50% less than yours looks to be totaled sweetheart !" I walked out of there and said in a whisper LOOKING UP,

"Oh hush!"

MAY 28:

I miss you DJB

MAY 30:

Dear Dennis:

I talked to God today and told him I miss you so very much. But instead of sadness I felt a sense of calm and I could picture you busy, and joyful and taking care of the business of the day. I am not sure if you have any pull with the angels but WE have a few friends that need some protection, guidance, and healing, so while I pray for them I want you to throw in a good word if you will. I know you are with me honey. Always, Debra

MAY 30:

Dear Dennis:

You know all those times you said—all those things—and I said you were wrong—well . . . . you were right !!! Sorry hon . . . I see it now !! I love you . . . djb

HE GOES WHEN I GO DEBRA

If you are a petite, small boned woman like myself (that's ok you can wipe up the coffee you just spit out later), then you know when you go into a store like Target or Wal-Mart and you shop for clothes there is a bit of discrimination taking place.

Let's say you wish to purchase a shirt or a nightgown. It comes in SM, MED, and LG. This item may be priced generally around $8.99. Ok, but then you realize that there is no way that even the LG size would cover your right hip or left breast. Do not fret, do not worry . . . there is a man out there that I like to call "Mr. X man". He has single handed figured out how my curves and stunning vivacious figure can look just as good as little Miss Size SM. He has a system, the "X system" and it goes like this . . .

1X = pretty as a picture and used to rock a Size LG but like the rest of us the years have caught up with you

2X = you are the bit more sturdily built yet fashionable woman of today, you are not afraid to show those curves

3X = you are stunning and beautiful but not ashamed to say even your right third toe over is not a Size MED. (that's not an insult ladies, I have been there)

And so on . . .

Ok, well apparently the difference between the LG and anything that ends in X requires a cost increase of approximately $2.00 because Mr. X Man stayed up all night working on this system, and come on girls, he has to feed his family somehow.

For years, when I picked out an item, I would have to buy a 1X or 2X depending on the level of stress in my life that year. I personally wanted to add this additional cost to the itemized list of money my EX owed me . . . you see why I hold him responsible right? Anyway where was I? This small sum was an "EXTRA FLUFF FEE" as my sweet loving husband Dennis would say. Of course when he tried to apply his "man logic" to the subject matter . . . "Wouldn't it just be cheaper to not buy the cheeseburger, lose the weight and pay $8.99?" . . . things would go downhill rapidly from there. No, he didn't ever put me down because of my weight and he told me all the time that I was pretty and beautiful, but he had his "man" moments needless to say. Men . . . they just don't get it. They seem to buy a larger size waist in jeans each year and if their belly gets bigger (which is the only place I swear they gain weight) it's not an issue because we all know their belly isn't going IN the jeans anyway.) So for every "extra fluff fee" remark that I tallied I secretly said . . . "honey I love you but someday . . . payback is a . . ."

OK my friend, you may be gone but Karma works on the deceased as well.

Dennis was 5'10 and approximately 250 lbs. when he died. He was a big guy, a man's man and I loved every cell of his dear sweet DNA but for all of the teasing I took over that extra $2.00 "fluff fee", I do believe I got my payback when it came time to purchase his URN.

First let me take you back to the funeral home where Timothy and I were led into a small room with nothing but urns displayed on small shelves. Each urn had a price tag in front of it to let you know right up front that you would need to sell your first born child (That was Tim by the way), a small farm animal or that treadmill you only were using as a clothing rack in your bedroom, because honey, 'sparing no expense" came at a cost.

Now to appreciate the predicament that Timothy and I were in to select this urn you need to understand Dennis just a bit further. This was the man who said, "I do not want to be buried in the ground because who will come to my grave after you and the kids are gone and then I will be stuck in the ground and my stone will not be taken care of and it will fall over and all you will have is this big stone lying in the dirt, because God knows it takes a lot of cement to spell B-u-j-a-n-o-w-s-k-I, and I just won't have that . . . Soooooooooooo . . . have me cremated and put into an urn until you decide where you are going to be and then we can have our ashes spread together (he must have forgotten my promise to be spread under the Health & Beauty Aids section of a new Wal-Mart or he would have never said that, I promise you) or I want part of me over the Daytona 500, part over Niagara Falls, and part over the Buffalo Bills stadium, not that this will help them win the Super Bowl. but . . ." Oh my GOD, I thought about burying him alive the day we had this conversation but my love for his big polish heart saved him once again.

With that said, Timothy and I set out to find an urn. I assure you the Funeral Director was doing his very best to "sell" us something "lovely, timeless and appropriate" but we were not having it. I was walking around this room looking at price tags that started at $600 and went up quite high from there. Now I assure you I would have again, "spared no expense" for this item as for Dennis I would have given or done anything, but at the same time I wanted to be sure I was making "good financial choices" which was the number one thing my husband respected in life. What was the next thing he respected in life? Men being men, no girly girl stuff. This is good to know . . . keep reading.

I took the walk slowly around this room with my 17 year old "boy" who would be turning 18 in just days and was now being the "man of the family" and helping his Mother do something that was so heart breaking and that neither of us thought we would ever have to do. Tim and I looked at urns which most had flowers, some with oriental designs, many looked like urns yet some were urns in disguise and looked like clocks. For the longest time the only words spoken in this room was the occasional "take your time and let me know if you have any questions" from the ever present Funeral Director which for some reason gave me the sense that he had been a "car salesman" in a previous life. I only remember not finding anything that struck me as "Dennis" and wondering what I should do, when suddenly the answer came to me. Yes there it was . . . the answer . . . in the form of a 17 year old (his filter was broke) boy who knew and loved his Step-Dad so well. He stated rather loudly, "OH MY GOD MOM, if we spend that much of Dennis' money on an urn with FLOWERS he is going to come down out of the sky and either strike us dead now or haunt us for the rest of our lives . . . (pause) . . . No FREAKIN' wayyyyyyyyyy !" No really, the blush on my face was PRIDE. He was so right and that was it for me . . . he had summed up what I was thinking entirely. I said, "Sir place my husband in a temporary urn and let me know when he is ready, we will take it from there." (Timothy, hon, I know for a fact that Dennis was up there at that very moment smiling down proudly saying, "That's my boy!")

So now where did this leave me? URN-less. I came home and began my search of the internet. Again I wanted something that said "Dennis" something that was tasteful but represented the man that he was and the person that we loved. You would be surprised what you can find on the internet when you search for urns but I struck gold. I came across a company that has handmade wooden urns of maple with the most beautiful carved designs and pictures on the front. I looked through all of the selections and there it was . . . it had the ducks flying overhead (the only hunting he loved to do), trout jumping out of the water (his favorite fishing that we did in North Carolina whenever we had the chance), two people on the water in a canoe (just the two of us), the mountains in the background (we spent every minute free as close to the mountains as we could get from the day we came to the Carolinas), it was so tasteful, classy, so nicely done and so . . . Dennis.

I made up my mind, I pulled out my credit card, I decided on what wording I wanted on the front (Loved deeply—Missed truly—Remembered forever). The purchase price was $180.00, and I thought, ok it's just what I wanted, he would really like this, it has everything that speaks of him, and this is the right thing to do. Since I am one of those "read the fine print" kind of gals, I did just that and this is what it said, "holds 200 C.I." Ok, I am sorry I was never good in math or science so C.I. was not registering for a moment. I click on the tab and it said, 1 C.I. (Cubic Inch) = 1 lb. Hmmm? Now I understand. Dennis weighing approximately 250 lbs. WOULD NOT FIT IN THIS URN. Well, what do you know? I then click on the drop down and choose 250-280 C.I. instead. Guess what? Yep, you got it . . . a $90.00 "EXTRA FLUFF FEE" because he was 50 lbs. over the weight limit for a "LG"! Oh my gosh did I laugh . . . .

I said to Dennis right out loud, "OK baby, I realize not buying the cheeseburger won't help you now, but I think we just became even on this one !!!"

You may think the story ended there but there is one more thing I wish to share with you about this urn. Due to the fact that Dennis was now 30 C.I.'s short of filling the space, placing him in there and leaving such a big gap gave me pause. (Bad joke inserted here) No it actually gave me "paws". On our dresser was yet another urn. This one was very small. It held the remains of Dennis' best friend Sabbath (Black Sabbath) his 16 year old black lab that he loved more than me I am certain. (It's ok, I am a dog freak, I get that.) Sabbath passed the year we moved to South Carolina and Dennis insisted that we have him cremated; his ashes carried home with us, and kept on our dresser in an urn covered in very tasteful velvet.

As the years passed, each time I would dust the "dresser and Sabbath" I would say as lovingly as possible, "Honey how long is this dog going to be on our dresser?" to which he always replied, "He goes when I go Debra!"

OK, then . . . all final wishes granted. Sabbath who appeared to be about a good 30 C.I.'s in remains was placed respectfully in the urn with his beloved master. They are resting happily in peace together now, side by side as in life, and you know it was almost as if God orchestrated the entire thing . . . it was the perfect fit!

JUNE 2012

(Facebook daily posts)

Summer Lovin' Happen So Fast

JUNE 1:

I sent an email to every one of Tim's teacher as extra security and said, "What is Tim's grade on his final exam and for your class?" Psychology teacher of Tim's sends email:

"Dear Mom, Tim got an 87 on his final exam so he is definitely passing this class."

This was one of Tim's harder classes so I wrote back to her and said, "Thank you Jesus." Apparently Tim was standing next to her when my email popped up as this was the reply:

"Hey Mom it's Tim. HE helped but I studied like you said I never do ! LOL"

JUNE 1:

Dear U.S. Army:

My son will be joining you soon. I know you are going to teach him to be all he can be, however, I have but one small favor to ask . . . Please make out his first 3 paychecks to "Bank of Mom". Thanks—I knew you would understand !!! Sincerely, Bank President and CEO/Mom

JUNE 3:

Good Sunday Morning friends . . . . I am excited as this morning will be my first visit to a new church with a new friend. Better than sitting at home stuck in our old ways and not making any changes or trying anything new. Dennis was never like that . . . he always wanted to go see something new and try new food and places. I refuse to sit here and let life happen to me. I have much to do before I meet up with him in eternity and I want the list of things to talk about to be long. Have a blessed day.

JUNE 3:

Church was about the book of Joshua today and how he and Caleb never wavered in their faith and God therefore blessed them. It was about no matter what adversity you face, no matter what heartache you walk through if you REFUSE to lose faith in the Lord you will be brought through to the other side where the sun shines and blessings abound. You think . . . It's almost like God knew I was there and made that preacher speak just to me.

JUNE 4:

Dear Dennis:

I woke with you on my mind today. This week is so filled with activity surrounding Tim's Graduation and family and friends coming. I know how changing your "normal" was never your thing and I was the one who got giddy with making all of the details and moments come together. At the end you were always proud and always happy as I know you would be this coming Saturday. I miss you so very much it just doesn't seem to be that words any longer cover how this feels. I will make you proud this week and I will be sure to give you much praise for all that you did to get Tim and all of us this far !!! Loving you always, Debra

JUNE 4:

People are really pissing me off today. Straight up.

JUNE 5:

He always said he didn't know how to be a parent, but was just doing the best he could. We made mistakes and we dealt with a lot of things that you usually don't unless divorce/custody is involved. Dennis was a big kid at heart. He loved to play, he loved electronics and toys and the kids NEVER wanted Mom to pick out the Christmas presents because "Dennis is great at that Mom, but you? Well no." He always looked for the toy that HE would have wanted to play with when it was Tim's gift and for Sarah (yes he even picked hers) he wanted her to have "what no other little girl had". He loved those kids so much and while he "didn't always know how to be a parent" he knew how to love, to protect, to provide, to teach and to guide. Saturday, OUR son Tim will walk across a stage and while that makes any Mom shed a few tears it is especially hard for me knowing that he is not here (yes I believe he will be with us in spirit) but you know what I mean. This was the moment he worked so hard for with Timothy. It is now Tim's turn to stand up and be a man. I pray God blesses Tim with many years, much success and happiness and tons of babies of his own (that's for me lol) but if he doesn't I pray he allows Tim to be the Dad "he didn't have to be" to another child like Dennis was to him.

JUNE 6:

Dear Dennis: I love you . . . I want you home, I want you here and I want to hug you. That's about as simple as it gets right now. Always, Debra

JUNE 8:

Dear Dennis:

Here we go !!! I am taking you with me each minute of the way !! I love you !!

JUNE 10: (What would have been Dennis' 47th birthday)

I made it all day without looking at a calendar. I wish I would have made it through to tomorrow. Today is Dennis' birthday. It would have been his 47th. Today is also the 4th year in which we took legal custody of the kids. Honey if I could shout loud enough, cry hard enough, scream long enough so you could hear me I would but that won't get me through to you I know. So instead, I send my prayers up to the Lord and ask him to deliver a special message just for you. All of my love forever . . . Debra

JUNE 11:

Dear Dennis:

I saw a place today that was so YOU. It was vast, flat, lush and green. A river ran through this place with amazing beautiful trees lining the water's edge. It also had a creek running through the other way . . . and the grass looked like the owner clipped each blade perfectly with a nail clipper. It was so beautiful it really took my breath away. Tim and I agreed you would have LOVED it. There was even a little bridge going over the creek that was rustic and sweet. I closed my eyes so you could see it too ! ♥ you . . . djb

JUNE 12:

Dear Dennis:

Before you died I said things like "I can't imagine life without you" and yet now I am living it. Now that you have died I say things like "I can't imagine you being gone longer than a few weeks" and yet now it's been nearly 9 months. Every morning I open my eyes you consume my first thoughts and every night my last. How long will this go on? I saw the movie Phenomenon with John Travolta (remember how I oooh'd and ahhhh'd over him and you would laugh at me). He found out he was dying soon in this movie and said to his girlfriend, "Will you love me for the rest of my life?" and she said, "No, but I will love you for the rest of mine!" Someone mentioned this movie to me recently and seeing it I remembered watching it with you. I am sure at the time we thought those lines to be very corny . . . yet now they answer the question . . . how long? For the rest of mine !!! ♥ Djb

JUNE 13:

Dear Dennis:

I made some decisions about ME, for ME, which will affect ME. I am not changing my mind, nor am I going to apologize to anyone, nor offer an explanation. I am doing this to make myself happy. If it comes off as selfish then my response is . . . "So, you get it hey?" I miss you so much and I know as sure as I am sitting here that you would be ok with this because why? Because you loved me. ♥ djb

JUNE 14:

Dear God:

I don't know what your plan is for me but please give me a clue . . . You know me (ha) when I am left to my own free will, I WILL bust a move and think of something to go for or try next. Sometimes that is good, sometimes it ends with "what was I thinking?" I am sitting on "GO" here waiting for you to reveal the next path/idea/plan. Meanwhile I believe in you, give you all the glory and praise I can and try to not let my "free will" outsmart my common sense! Sincerely, Your child in waiting ♥ djb

P.S. If you consult Dennis he will just tell you I was never really good at listening so . . . you may want to give that consideration when trying to reach me !! I ♥ +

JUNE 14:

Dear Dennis:

What I wouldn't give to climb into your big strong arms, lay my head on your chest and hang on for the rest of my days. I pray you are in a state of joy so profound that you couldn't stop smiling if you tried. I pray that you are light and free and can no longer describe things like anger, pain or sorrow if called upon to do so. I pray that what you remember of your time here is filled with snapshots of love, laughter and tenderness only. I pray that fear and worry have no ability to exist in your forever home. I pray that you know somehow that there was one Father that has always loved you unconditionally and you are with HIM now. I pray that you know I WILL climb into your strong arms again one day, I WILL lay my head on your chest and for the rest of OUR days in eternity we will just . . . be. ♥ djb

JUNE 14:

Dear Dennis:

I just saw an O'Charleys commercial and I couldn't stop giggling. You remember when we lived in Jax and we went out to dinner one night to try this new place that just opened. You were so stunned that I, Debra Jane "let's not rock the boat in public" Blood returned 2, not 1 but 2 meals before I got something I liked. (Naturally I was polite when I did this but . . .) They kept saying, "Is everything ok? Do you like your meal?" and I kept saying, "Nope sure don't, bring me . . . .". You said, "I can't believe you keep returning your meal." I told you that if I didn't like it why should I keep it, pay for it and just pretend that it was good. You said quite smart like . . . "so you are just going to keep returning meals until you get the one you like, is that how you handle things MISSY?" To which I said, "Shoot I would return you if you weren't so dang cute and I knew where the return counter was !" I swear to this day you tilted your head like Mocha, as you were not quite sure as to whether I meant that or not !! I don't know why that stuck with you so much but I must have heard "Do you know what Debra did one time when I took her to dinner?" a billion times if I heard it 10. You know we served as each other's entertainment on most given days !! lol ♥ djb

JUNE 18:

Dear Dennis:

You think you didn't have a ripple effect in this life? I called the pool store (the one that we used to replace the liner) and while I was identifying myself he asked for my phone number. I gave it and YOUR name came up. The minute he saw your name he got all excited and said, "OH I REMEMBER YOUR HUSBAND HE WAS HILARIOUS . . . HE TOLD ME ONE OF THE FUNNIEST JOKES I HAVE EVER HEARD !!!" He was very sad to hear that you had passed and said, "I will send one of my guys out there to help you and I am going to give you a discount for Dennis". I told him that was not necessary and I did not expect anything of the sort but he was insisting. He said, "No let me do it for him . . . I know he would want you taken care of !!" Bless him, what a sweet man. See babe . . . some man you met once and he remembers you with a smile !!! That's what my love for you was all about !!! ♥ djb

JUNE 18:

Dear Dennis:

This is why she is YOUR girl. She ate Salmon tonight and loved it (you insisted on fish once a week), she fed the dogs on time and I just heard the LAWNMOWER start up . . . that girl is on a John Deere! Aren't you proud?

JUNE 19:

Dear Dennis:

Good Morning baby. If you were here I would have already handed you your cup of morning coffee and provided your first hug. I sure do miss you. I picture you happy and patting that belly of yours with each laugh. Remember you used to say we would never leave each other because "who else would have us". LOL. They can call me crazy but I believe you never really completely left. I am the keeper of "what was Dennis J. Bujanowski". I somehow feel that it's my job to keep your memory alive because no one loved or knew you more. Others miss you yes, but in the year following your passing I want the world to know what a special person you were. Sure you had some flaws but don't we all. What if we left this world and no one remembered us or talked about the mark we left on their lives? I would find that so sad. Well you left a huge impact on our lives and we love to laugh at what was "you", we love to talk about our time with you, and we pray that you hear each word and feel each hug and prayer we send your way. Always, ♥ djb

JUNE 20:

Dear Dennis:

I read my daily devotional today which is written as if Jesus were the actual one speaking to you. It said, "I speak to you continually. My nature is to communicate, though not always in words." Then . . . "You can find Me in each moment, when you have eyes that see and ears that hear." Then . . . "Gradually you will find Me in more and more of your moments." Then . . . "You will seek Me and find Me, when you seek Me above all else." Well, for those that think it's a bunch of **Hooey**, I am here to say . . . it's not . . . it's true. When you open your heart to listen with more than your ears, and see with more than your eyes, you will find HIM. He is always with us, always. So, Dennis knowing that you are with Jesus, and He is always with us means simply what? . . . . Right . . . In a beautiful way we are still together. God gave me free will. I use mine to remain closer to God and you. Always, ♥ djb

JUNE 22:

Dear Dennis:

Would you be doing the same if it was me that left that day? Would I consume so much of your thoughts? Would you be praying for my soul? Would you still wonder if I was ok even though you knew I was in the safest hands possible? I filled up your truck with gas this morning. Stopping at the convenience/gas station made me think of all of those road trips to NY and FL. Sarah was with me and we said, "Yep he would have pumped the gas and sent us in for a purple Gatorade". Just simple everyday moments hold you in them. You are a part of every memory, and while I know without wanting to realize it we are making new memories without you . . . there will never be a day for me without you in it . . . no matter where this life takes me as I wind my way back to you. Always, ♥ djb

JUNE 22:

If it weren't for my broken heart, I believe I would be the happiest person alive !

JUNE 23:

Dear Dennis:

OK, hang onto your cloud there honey. I took a chance and I joined Christianmingle. com. It's a dating site for Christians. No I won't run off with a guy named Hernando to Brazil and leave the kids . . . (not just yet anway lol). Anyhow . . . there is a man a few years younger than me, who lives nearby and he actually emailed me. Do you want to know what we talked about? Ok, get ready . . . this is pretty hot stuff now . . . TURKEY HUNTING, FISHING AND LABS !!! Yep, there you have it !!! So far I have determined he would be the PERFECT DATE FOR MY BROTHER but I will let you know how it turns out for me !!! I hear you . . . I AM careful and cautious but don't want the dust to get 3" thick on me while I sit around crying over myself you know? I know you are supporting all that I do AND want me happy. I am also certain that I may never find another because I have to let go of that "measuring up to Dennis" thing to make that happen. I will check back in with you soon honey . . . be sure to check with God for your daily message from me!! I love you always, ♥ djb

JUNE 23:

In the year since Dennis has passed, I will have made 3 plane trips, 1 road trip to Florida, had surgery (elective), graduated a son, moved a daughter to her senior year, had a new roof, deck and plumbing done, bought his car, joined a church, lost weight and inches, had highlights put in my hair, graduated a son from basic training, wrote many chapters to my book, grew in my faith with Jesus Christ, and probably many more things that I am not thinking of or haven't happened just yet. In the words of a Reba song, "Life won't stop for my broken heart!" When they say God has a plan for your life . . . the biggest thing you need to understand I am guessing is that it's HIS plan and while your free will certainly plays a part . . . I would have NEVER made it this far without God or all of you !!!

JUNE 24:

So the phone rang at midnight. I was just getting ready to chew someone out for calling my house so late and then I hear "Mom? It's Tim!" Ok, that scared me to death but he is fine and was being SMART and using the brain he has to stay out of trouble and make good decisions. Thank you Dennis for watching over him . . . I knew you would hear me.

JUNE 24:

I am wide awake watching PRETTY WOMAN with Richard Gere and Julia Roberts and it made me miss being in love. While Dennis was not a billionaire and I was not a hooker HAAAAAAAAAAAAAAAAAAA . . . . It still brought back some sweet memories !!! Miss you my love, miss you so much.

JUNE 25:

Dear Dennis:

I miss you today baby . . . I wish I could hug the daylights out of you. Praying your soul is resting in peace each and every minute that we are apart. ♥ djb

JUNE 26:

Dear Dennis:

There isn't a day that goes by that I don't call upon something you taught me, an example you set, an idea that you shared. You were such a driving force in this family and I am truly grateful for the good days as well as the bad days we had. I seriously would not trade a minute. Today I give thanks to God for this time we shared. Missing you always ♥ djb

JUNE 27:

Dear Dennis:

Were you trying to reach me this morning? It played. Our song. It was "There's no way I could make it without you, there's no way that I'd even try . . . if I had to survive without you in my life, I know I wouldn't last a day . . ." Sound familiar? It was the song you had played as I walked down those steps to take your hand in marriage. It played on the way to take Sarah to school this morning. I could see you standing there so strong and handsome in your suit. I remember the look we had the moment we saw each other that day. Yes, of course the tears fell because I miss you so much and I can't see you but I know that I am one of the most blessed women alive . . . as I was Mrs. Dennis James Bujanowski. P.S. Those "3 in a row" Rolling Stones songs on the return trip were just to make me smile again right? I love you always, ♥ djb

JUNE 27:

MY DAILY DEVOTIONAL TODAY READS: Rest with ME a while. You have journeyed up a steep, rugged path in the recent days. The way ahead is shrouded in uncertainty. Look neither behind you nor before you. Instead focus your attention on ME, your constant companion. I designed time as a protection for you. You couldn't bear to see all your life at once. Though I am unlimited by time, it is in the present moment that I meet you. Thank you Jesus—these words bring me such peace.

JUNE 30:

I love you Dennis . . . wish you were here!

I AM DARTH VADAR

When I first thought of telling this story my initial thought was that if you hadn't seen *Star Wars* all those years ago, this would not be funny to you, but then I thought . . .

There are moments in every married couple's lives that maybe you shouldn't share with others, as it may be one of those, "let's keep that just between us shall we?" However because of the comedic value in the moment there is just no way you cannot.

Dennis and I had those moments time and again and that is what made our days together so *Dennis & Debra.* I have always been quick witted and "funny" according to friends, and to my husband, well, he always said . . . "you are a nerd Debra Blood!" While that may be true in part Dennis had a sense of humor "all his own". He was extremely funny, yet not always on the surface. It was sort of a "when you least expected it" type of thing. He always seemed to be serious, but then something would come out of his mouth that would make you wish you had a coupon for Depends undergarments. What made him so funny was really that . . . he didn't always know he was.

Let me share with you one my favorite "Dennis" moments . . .

One weekend, while living in Jacksonville, Florida at the first home that we ultimately shared and was the official first "love nest", Dennis invited over his best friend to hang out as they often did. This particular weekend my sister-in-law came to visit as she had some other business is town so she was able to stay with us for the night. We all gathered around the bar (Dennis' homemade bar in our house which served as a memorial to Dale Earnhardt Sr.), just the four of us. We listened to our favorite music, had a few drinks as we "shot the $#@$" as they say. The conversation turned into a female vs. male point of view discussion back and forth on several different topics. We were all giving our individual, "single" status, blatantly honest perspectives on whatever topic came up next.

There were adult based questions being thrown out as you would find in a Cosmopolitan magazine, about religion, sex, drugs, dating, relationships, marriage, kids, etc. Keep in mind that we had had a few drinks in us and everyone was feeling free to speak openly, holding nothing back. I can't be sure who ask the question but I promise you I will never forget it . . .

When you have sex do you ever <u>think of</u> someone else?

Ok, that is what I heard. That is what Dennis' friend heard. That is what my sister-in-law heard, but let me tell you what the three of us heard coming from Dennis seconds later . . .

In a deep-throated raspy voice presented as his best Star Wars character impression . . . from Dennis we heard . . .

"I . . . AM . . . DARTH VADAR !!!"

So we all had to get up off the floor and put the chairs back where they were standing before we fell over in uncontrollable laughter. Once breathing had resumed for each of us again after a good 20 seconds or so and the tears had been wiped from our eyes, I realized <u>exactly</u> what Dennis had heard. I put my arm around him (more for support for myself as I couldn't stand up from laughing so hard) and said . . .

"Honey, (Oh dear God), Honey, the question was <u>NOT</u> **when you have sex do you think you <u>are </u>someone else, it was do you think <u>of</u> someone else? And let me add . . . good to know babe !"**

All I got from Dennis at that point was a priceless look, a slight pause and then one little, "Ha!"

From that point forward, each year Dennis was the proud recipient of a Darth Vadar item. He owned a lunchbox, a watch, a bobble-head for the car, a necktie . . . no I couldn't let it go. I told him I would NEVER role-play and dress as "Princess Anybody" and until the day he died anytime we saw Darth Vadar on TV or referenced in anything, we would just give each other "that" look and begin to laugh.

While I promise you we never shared this story with the kids, it was only years later when another moment in time brought this Darth Vadar story full circle. Tim and Sarah were on the floor wrestling as brother and sister will at times do. They had been giggling while at the same time trying to punch the snot out of each other, for the lack of a better description. Sarah was on top and had Tim pinned to the ground when . . .

In a deep-throated raspy voice presented as his best Star Wars impression . . . from Tim we heard . . .

"LUKE, I AM YOUR FATHER!"

While they may have been "Step-Father and Step-Son" apparently when the galaxies align just right . . .

JUST BETWEEN US

Do you have girl friends that go out each week and get their nails done? Spend every other weekend with friends for a "girl's night out", go shopping with their BFF or belong to a club that they spend time attending with their friends? Do you have a guy friend that goes golfing or fishing with the guys, has a night out on the town after work, works on cars or attends sporting events with "the guys?"

That was not us!

From day one we were together every minute that God allowed. Of course I want to say it's because we loved each other, and we did, but we never left each other's side. Up until 9/25/2011, the day God called him home, the most time that Dennis and I had spent apart in nearly 16 years was three weeks.

When his work had him attend training out of state for three weeks, we swore we would never be apart that long again. Oh how I wish that was a promise we could have kept. The one time that his work wanted him to be gone for two weeks to training in Ohio he had me take a week vacation and the kids and I went and stayed with him. We had a lot of fun on that trip. The kids and I used the pool at the hotel during the day and then at night it was like coming home to our family but just in a new house with a different town to explore.

Dennis was all "male" and by that I mean, he said things like, "Debra you should really go find something to do." "You should get out of the house more.", "Why don't you call your friends and go do something?" But I promise you . . . the minute I even thought of doing one of those things . . . the other side of Dennis came out. The puppy dog, "What? Are you leaving me?" look hit his face. "How long are you going to be gone?" was always the next question. No he was not possessive; he just hated to be without his wife and me without my husband. We were best friends, BFFs, inseparable from day one and we liked it that way . . . we hated to be apart, we missed each other if we were apart for 24 hours. I missed him when he went to work for the day. God forbid we went a day without talking to each other at least once during the workday. It was just the way we were. We didn't try to hide it. We didn't apologize for it. We thought this was what "married couples" were supposed to do.

Did we drive each other crazy when we were together? Sure we did, we were married. We argued and annoyed each other, got tired of each other, went to our separate areas of the "house" but I promise you rarely did we get any further apart than that. All vacations were together, when one of us had to stay in the hospital the other one was there. If he wanted to go fishing, I brought along my crochet, cross-stitch or books and rested on the bank or in the truck while he "reeled in the big ones" and then I served as the official photographer for every "big" catch. Together, always . . . We were "Dennis & Debra" not Dennis and then Debra. We were "US" that is how we wanted it to be.

Now that he is gone I wonder if losing him would have been easier if we were the couple that spent more time out with friends than at home together. I know in my heart I would not trade one single moment of those years to make this pain end now. God knows how I loved my best friend and God truly knows how much I miss him today.

I wish I could remember the year, but sometime between 2001-2005 Dennis had a big event occur in his life. He and his best (guy) friend got tickets to see his favorite band in concert . . . The Rolling Stones in Atlanta, GA. Talk about excited. Oh, my gosh. It was as if he had won the lottery. He talked non-stop about this for weeks. He owned every CD of theirs. He knew every song. He could "name that tune" in two notes. He bragged to me and said "I bet you wish you could go" when in fact I really was not a Stones fan (we shall speak of my love for Jon Bon Jovi in a moment). I only listened to them with him because that was "his thing". One of those things you share out of your love for another.

He said more than once he "couldn't wait to get away and have some guy time." Guy time? Oh yes, the guys had a plan. They were going to drive from Jacksonville, FL to Atlanta, GA (not that far) attend the concert, stay in a hotel and come home the next day. It was "just an overnighter Debra, you won't even have time to miss me." Miss you? I have my new book, my movie rentals, the dogs, favorite fast food so I don't have to cook. I have my comfy pjs on, and I am ready for a night that is all about ME. I am going to relax, clean NOTHING, read a little, take a long hot bath and just enjoy the peace and quiet of having the house to myself. That's what I am going to do Dennis! That's what I am going to do right up until the time the phone rings and I hear . . .

HUNDREDS OF SCREAMING VOICES, BLARING MUSIC that sounds somewhat like Gimme Shelter *our* favorite Stones song. Through all of this "noise" I faintly make out what is to be my sweet husband's screaming voice yelling, "Debra can you hear that? It's them! I am right next to the stage! I am looking right at Mick—Oh My God, can you hear that Debra?"

Would you believe me if I told you that for the next 2 hours I stayed on the phone with Dennis and I can now actually say (in a sense) "I have been to a Rolling Stones concert!" I lay on the floor with my head on a pillow to the "wee hours". I propped the phone on the pillow and put it on speaker phone. I made sure all the phones in the house were charged as I switched them out every other "set" that "the band" played. I laughed at him, I gave up trying to talk to him early on because he couldn't hear me, but I could hear him. "Isn't this awesome babe?" he would scream. "You love this song don't you?" "I wish you could see this, you wouldn't believe it!" All night, the entire concert, amazingly his cell phone battery never died and WE attended the concert . . . TOGETHER. When he hung up that night ironically enough he said, "You know I miss you!" Really honey, it almost feels like we were never apart! When I teased him after he came home about how I never really got a chance to "miss him", I just got a big Dennis hug, a kiss on my forehead, and a "Glad you went with me babe!"

So now you know that Dennis was a hard rocking Stones fan to the end, but me . . . I was more into the "Hair Bands" of the 80's. Well actually I was just more into Bon Jovi. Well to be completely truthful, I am STILL into Bon Jovi, this really is not a "past tense" thing. I told my husband that the ONE thing I MUST do before I die is see Bon Jovi. Dennis worked for a large healthcare company and as it happened, this company's name was put on the Arena in Atlanta. When tickets went on sale the employees would get an email listing sent to them. Let the world stop turning . . . Bon Jovi was coming to Atlanta GA—*April 15, 2010*-and my man was getting tickets! I can't begin to tell you how many "points" he knew he had earned for making this happen but he was very secure in his ranking as a recipient for the "Husband of the Year" award.

The following is an excerpt of my posting from my favorite social media wall the day after what would be one of the most amazing nights of my life. While I put no other (here on earth) above my husband during our entire marriage, I must admit I not so secretly held Mr. Bon Jovi pretty darn high up there as well. As you can see that even though the evening was about Mr. JBJ . . . it was Dennis who was "in the spotlight" the next day.

Post April 16, 2010

Good Morning my fellow Bon Jovi supporters: I made it. I didn't pass out. I did almost cry but not quite. I did not pee myself (for all of you who had your money on that one) however Dennis was texting home telling the kids "Bon Jovi is taking the stage. Mom to pee herself soon . . . more to come." OMG he is too funny. Was it awesome? OMG yes !!!! Is he beautiful? OMG beyond that !!!! He was great . . . he is SO full of energy and really gave the show his all, you could tell.

My friend who I worked with was directly across the stadium from me but we couldn't get to each other. We talked on the phone and stood up and waved to each other (it was pretty funny) and said things like, "OMG HE is going to be on THAT stage in just minutes OMG !!" Yeh, it was very TEEN like.

Then he took the stage. Can you believe I can't tell you the first song he played because 1/ it was a new one and 2/ I think I was in shock!!! I tried to get pictures but it was so dark and very hard to get them.

I loved *"It's my life"* and *"Someday Saturday Night"*. Did I mention how sexy and beautiful he is? OMG that man just gets better with age. I think I heard him say, "This one is for you Debra" but I am sure that was only in my head!

Now, let me tell you about my AWESOME husband . . . first LOVE YOU DENNIS SO MUCH . . . for getting the tickets, making this all happen. LOVE YOU LOVE YOU LOVE YOU . . . . That was my dream come true besides spending my life with you baby!

Back to my story . . . We ended up in the club section . . . the first thing I hear him (Dennis—Mr. Sports Fan . . . Mr. Buffalo, N.Y.) say . . . "COOL they have a bar and a big screen . . . I CAN get through this !" This made me laugh. *He is not a Bon Jovi fan . . . he is a Debra fan!! That is the sweetest part.*

So he went down to the section with me and sat in the seat, listened to the opening band and he was there for like the first TWO songs of JBJ but . . . . You know how at concerts EVERYONE stands up practically the WHOLE TIME??? Well Dennis was the only one sitting down. He really does not get into Bon Jovi at all but he was there for me so I couldn't complain.

Anyway the man next to Dennis thought maybe he was in Dennis' way or something so he tapped him on the shoulder and said, "You ok, can you see, don't you like this guy?"

Dennis said, "No man, it's cool I AM TAKING ONE FOR THE TEAM !!" The guy dies laughing and says, "DUDE WE ARE ALL TAKING ONE FOR THE TEAM!!" OMG MEN !!! After that Dennis went to the club section, drank beer and watched Buffalo Sabres hockey! Sabres WON by the way and Dennis was thrilled! He sent me text messages every so often with . . . 'you okay? Still peeing yourself?" But that is where he spent the entire concert!!! Ahhhhh gotta love it.

Sincerely,

JBJ's biggest fan !!!!

Some of the responses I got were really not so much about Jon as they were . . . well . . .

- Sounds most wonderful. Glad you finally got to see him. **Dennis** is an awesome guy.

- OMG you are soooooooooo hilarious!!!!

  I SO love that **Dennis** "took one for the team" LOL!!

  It sounds like you had the best night ever! I'm so happy for you! I loved every word of your recap . . . especially when he dedicated the song to you lmao!! Glad you had the best time ever!!

- **Dennis** is THE MAN!!!

- I am so jealous that you got to see him. LOL But I am so happy for you! I believe he dedicated a song to you!!!!! We looked on line last night to see if he was coming to our town but he is not. I am so glad you got to go and **Dennis** is a great guy for taking one for the team!!!!!

- I would have sobbed my way thru Hallelujah!!! You are one lucky girl and kudos to **Dennis** for being a "Debra fan" sure would like to meet this guy someday.

- That is awesome! I am so glad you shared your entire experience with us . . . you are hysterical and **Dennis** is the man!

- I bet that bar looked like the benches at the mall. A bunch of guy's waiting on the wives/Girlfriends . . . . **Dennis** deserves MAJOR kudos for that 'gift' to Deb, for sure!

- I am beyond happy for you. Let me not forget to mention that I am also 'way' fond of **Dennis** for . . . well . . . being the man you have been meant to have all along.

- Thanks for sharing the whole experience with us.

  I remember the day you got the tickets; you listed the happiest days of your life, and now you are able to add another. Hang on to that **hubby**; he is responsible for some of the entries on that list of happiest days.

- I was thinking of you last night, hoping you were having a WONDERFUL time. **Dennis** ROCKS!!!

- I bet you sang all the songs . . . did you wave your lit up cell phone all around? I honestly got teary-eyed when you said **Dennis** is a "Debra fan" . . . what a super cool thing. Now what will you do to make it up to him?

- YEAH Blood . . . thanks so much for sharing this it's awesome . . . . I loved the "Debra fan" part too . . . cuz' I'm one too! Love you and that **man** of yours . . . so glad it was as awesome as you expected!

I started that morning as Jon Bon Jovi's biggest fan. I ended that evening as Dennis James Bujanowski's biggest idol. I was so exhausted at the end of the concert and I had no voice left. I remember walking up to him after the concert as he sat at the table in the club section. I fell into his arms and told him he was "the BEST husband that ever lived". I spent the ride home back to South Carolina, one eye open, head on his shoulder and every few miles I would smile and announce in my raspy squeaky voice . . . "Oh my Gosh do you know how much I love you?"

He knew.

JULY 2012

(Facebook daily posts)

Fireworks In My Heart

JULY 4:

Dear Dennis:

I love you and miss you more than words can say. Do you remember all of the crazy fun we had with fireworks each year? It started with them being so little they were only allowed to hold sparklers while singing patriotic songs and it built into Tim hiding behind a large object and you shooting small fireworks his way. I objected, you two laughed and said "Chill Mom" as each year you guys tried to make them bigger, louder and more spectacular.

JULY 5:

Let me tell you how uplifted my heart has been over the last few weeks. I have had more phone calls with folks that I haven't talked to in years. I will forever be grateful for the love and support and kindness of each of you that have reached out to me, and truly "been there for me" during this time. May I be a blessing to you in return in some way in this life. Love you all.

JULY 5:

Dear Dennis:

When I look at this picture it makes me think of late fall/early winter in Oceanway, Jacksonville, FL. In 2001 just a week before Christmas we signed the papers on our new home that held 2-3 acres and a mobile home and garage. Yes we moved from a much larger home into a smaller mobile home but it was the land and the open space that we were seeking. To be out in the country and have room to do things LIKE let Tim ride a dirt bike, let Sarah ride her bike, let the dogs run and have a campfire in our own back yard. I can still smell the cold crisp air of the day we walked into the house for the first time when we were given the keys. We didn't say a word. We followed each other from room to room taking in every inch of what was now ours. The only words spoken in the house that day were as we stopped and took one last look around before we left. You hugged me tight and said, "Are you happy babe?" Wasn't that always the question? Didn't you make every decision with that in mind? Of course the answer was yes, for I was with you. The house wasn't what made me happy. It was you, it was always you. God how I miss you and pray for your soul. Your loving wife, ♥ djb

JULY 6:

Dear Dennis:

You know I used to count on you so much for just about everything. I am sorry if I put such a huge burden on your shoulders. I was driving back from the Doctor's today by myself as the lady behind the counter told me a different "shorter" way to go. I knew that my friend had gone this way but I was drugged so I did not have this committed to memory. You remember how I always wanted you to drive, and I would never go somewhere that I was not familiar with . . . without you. I thought first . . . "no go with what you know" and then I thought of you. I could hear you saying, "No Debra, take a damn chance—you can do it!" (ha) so I turned towards unfamiliar . . . and when I hit 85 So. in just a couple of turns . . . I said out loud . . . "Yay Us !!". You really are always with me in a way I can't explain. I don't know if it's just that I want you to be or it's my imagination gone wild or spirits are for real . . . but I choose to believe in the spirit world and that you are gently guiding me through my days !!! Always, ♥ djb

JULY 7:

Dear Dennis:

I have a confession. Sometimes I try NOT to think about you because it hurts too much. Then I go for a couple of days and you pop into my mind and a wave of sadness hits me so hard. You would not have done well with this whole death thing. I see you yelling "Damn it Debra" every time you couldn't find something or the wave hit you. Men and women handle grief very differently. I know yours would have included VERY LOUD Rolling Stones music right? This promise of eternity and seeing each other again better be true because I will not be very happy if I get where I am going and you are not there. I miss you my love . . . always. ♥ djb

JULY 10:

Dear Dennis:

It is days like this . . . moments like this . . . when my tears won't stop falling, when my heart is broke. I would simply walk into a room, walk up to you, put my head on your chest, have a mini meltdown and you would hug me, tell me it was going to be ok, (or give me the "it is what it is Debra" speech), kiss my forehead and it would all be better. I remember asking you one day as you were done comforting me, "Will you do this too when we are old please?" You said, "That's what I signed up for baby". I get mad at God for taking you away at moments like this. I don't want to send my son off to basic without you there to keep me strong and together, I don't want to watch my daughter graduate or walk down the aisle without you to keep me calm, soothed and still standing. I am mad at God for this and you can tell him it's ok because I have. I miss you and your strength that you brought to this family. So, bottom line God . . . I don't want to do all of these things without Dennis, but I will. All my love, ♥ djb

JULY 11:

Dear Dennis:

In 14 days I will be getting on a plane and flying home to Michigan. How I wish you could go with me and enjoy the festivities. (Of course secretly you will be with me anyway right?) I want you to know that I have sent a prayer to heaven for you each and every day that you have been gone. I have prayed for your soul and sent you a message of love, each day different, each day special, with God as the messenger.

I pray that you have gotten all of them. It won't be long and we will be talking about how you have been gone a year. Truthfully, I wish I could stop time so it won't come and in another way I want to rush past the date so fast that we don't have time to think about that day so long ago. Missing you is natural, missing you is expected, but what I have also learned is that missing you is exhausting. I am tired. Having a broken heart wears you out like you couldn't imagine Dennis. I just keep thinking that you are the one in the glory of it all. You are the one with no pain, no worries, no stress or anger . . . you are living a life of joy and peace. That is not how I wanted it if I had a choice (you know what I mean), but since I don't, I want you to know that I will keep on missing you until I see you again . . . no matter how tired I get. Always, ♥ djb

JULY 12:

Dear Dennis:

Woke up with a bad headache and missing you. I don't know why it comes in waves like this. I can go weeks and be fine but then I can go days and not be good at all. They say there are different stages of grief, but I think there are different "phases" of grief. Yes there is denial, anger, etc. those are the stages but what they don't talk about so much is how even months later, probably years (as I will find) it will come at you again with a force that resembles Day #1 all over again. Only now the sadness is not about that fact that you died, it's more about not being able to remember the sound of your voice, your smell, your touch or your face clearly. It's that you could possibly fade from our memory and the fear of that happening. I remember I went through this with my Dad who died way back in 1988. Dad had a very distinctive voice. Years later my brother sent me tapes he found in the basement. These were of when Dad & Mom had moved to Florida and it was of Dad sending a cassette recording of himself talking to his brother's Rex and John back in MI, which was his way of communicating. I was warned before I listened to these that they were coming as they didn't want me to be upset hearing his voice again. I claimed of course that this would not be an issue and waited with much excitement for these to arrive. Let me tell you that the minute I pushed "play" and I heard my Dad the tears fell like Niagara Falls. I **had** forgotten his voice, how could this be? I can't tell you what it did for my heart to "hear" him again. His laugh, the way he talked about "Deb called tonight", etc. I live with the fear Dennis that this is happening again, but while I can't hear you speak out loud to us every day, it is with God's amazing grace that in my heart I still hear your voice. I still hear you saying "I love you baby doll." I pray you are hearing me too! Always, ♥ djb

JULY 15:

Dear Dennis:

I love you. I told you this every day that you were here so why should now be any different? Always, ♥ djb

JULY 16:

Dear Dennis:

As I am drinking my coffee this morning I am thinking of you. It is little things like . . . coffee. I have always drank my coffee black and you always had to have cream added. When we went on a road trip I would add creamer to the thermos because that is how you liked it even though I didn't. I always tried to put you first. Every now and then when I am missing you, I pour a hot cup of coffee and add the creamer. Can you imagine that there is comfort in that? I know you would think of that as silly. The little things.

There is the new heating and air vent that comes up through our closet that you had done. You covered it with brick paneling and when you open our closet that is what you see. You said, "Debra, don't be putting nails in there and hanging things on that". Sorry my love, there is now 1 nail. When I open the closet of all of MY things the first thing I see is YOUR Ducks Unlimited hat hanging on that one nail. The one you wore every day you were off work and what you had on when God called you home. The little things.

It's the little things, no . . . it is "ANY little thing" that keeps us close to you. We know we lost you that day but we choose not to lose you each day thereafter from our minds or our hearts, so we do things "the way Dennis would have." We keep certain items that would be insignificant to others in a specific place, we mimic your taste, ideas, and mannerisms just to have a little piece of you with us somehow. You were my world and as long as I live and breathe you must know that was . . . no little thing. Always, ♥ djb

JULY 17:

Dear Dennis:

I have about 8 days before I make my trip to MI, then I have a month and it's time to go to KC, then Tim leaves for basic training, Sarah goes back to school, Tim graduates basic and I have another trip in the fall for a wedding . . . life just does not slow down. I know I could hide away and grieve forever and I promise you that because I chose to open the door and walk into the sunshine somewhat sooner than expected does not mean I love you less or do not still mourn your loss. (Geesh honey do you not read my posts? lol) I just have never been one to give up, accept defeat, or let the bad things in life bring me down to the point I can no longer function. Oh yes, there are still those days when my pillow, a box of Kleenex and TV are all I need but they are not as frequent now.

The Bible says: "Blessed are they that mourn, for they shall be comforted." Matthew 5:4

See God has comforted me Dennis. He has helped me to see "life" as it is being lived so joyfully around me when all I could think of was death and loss. He has also let me know that you are still living just not as we know it here. I will see you again. I often think if you would just walk through that door and I could hug you one more time . . . that face, that smile, those arms stretched out to hold me, that is how I picture seeing you again. Until then I will keep sending you messages of love and prayers. Always, ♥ djb

JULY 17:

I would like to take a minute to say THANK YOU to James and Kris Conner offering to help me and this family. You are a true role model for your boys and such a blessing to this family. All my love, Deb, Timmy, Sarah Jane and "your" Grandma

JULY 18:

Dear Dennis:

Two things occurred yesterday that bring me to write to you these words this morning. One . . . I was ask "how did you and Dennis meet?" Well there's a loaded question hey? lol. I gave the play by play and it brought back the warm and fuzzy feelings of how I fell in love with the "man with the plan", such determination, such intelligence, incredible strength, and ok yes, very sexy and you had arms that wouldn't quit and oh how my heart would melt when I would walk in a room and you would smile so sweetly and greet me with "hey baby doll".

I was then talking to a young person yesterday about "the first three years of marriage" and how they are the most difficult and I basically said, "If you can make it through the arguments over $$ and silly things and the struggles for independence & freedom . . . it's how you handle those days that make you fall in love all over again when you are 40 or beyond." That was so true for us. Man we were stubborn and set in our ways but let another try to come between us and we built a wall that could not be penetrated by the strongest of forces.

It takes a commitment like no other to stand together and stand "the test of time" as they say. I always knew it would really be "till' death do us part" for us (yes there were days when I was sure it would be us killing each other—lol), but I never thought it would be so soon. I know if you had lived another 10, 20 or more years we would still be together, still holding up that wall and letting no one or thing break it down. We were such a team, you and I.

We were never perfect, and we sure didn't try to be but, I would like to think that before we were born God had made a big "Till' death do us part" list. On this list he placed those that would stand by each other no matter how hard the trials placed in front of them, or the mistakes and bad days lying behind them.

On this list God said, "I will place two souls that will be tried and tested and then tested again, two hearts that will never love another as they do each other, two that could never alone be what they are so wonderfully together, two people who will make a home, build a life, love children and give all of themselves to others while thanking ME each day that they can. I will place two individuals on this list who will know that the love they have for each other was truly something precious and not just "what happened" yet it was a "gift" from ME. I will place on my list, a man and a woman who had it specifically written in their own wedding vows, "I will leave this earth loving no other" . . . Yes, I like to think God said, "My list will show . . ."

TILL' DEATH DO US PART

1. Debra ♥ Dennis

2.

3.

Always, ♥ djb

JULY 20:

Dear Dennis:

I spoke to your Aunt last night and it is always so good to talk to someone that loved you like I did. You were so special to her and she says she thinks of you so very often. I got her caught up on the kids and what is going on these days and we talked about how we were so thankful for that last vacation in July to NY & MI. The one that you came home repeatedly referring to as "the best vacation we ever had".

We talked about how you saw your cousins, Aunt, Uncles, my hometown and yours. You took me to a special place that held one of your favorite childhood memories. I took you to a special place that overflowed with mine.

You met so many of my friends that you only knew through the words of my stories told a billion times. You spent 3 days on "my" lake fishing with my brother (the one that you never really ever had time with). You had time with Tim to be silly and laughed so hard when you said to him, "Did your Mom show you the picture of the fish I caught?" and he replied, "well I saw the pictures but actually I thought that was . . . the bait!"

We were so relaxed, and laughed easy. There was alone time with you fishing off the rocks while I watched from a few feet away, book and crafts in hand. No words, just a look or a smile every now and then.

Then we found that tiny pub and went in for a "cold beer" after a day in the sun. We walked in and there was a "Stones" song playing loudly and the first thing you saw was that neon "Molson" sign. You laughed and said, "Hmm Babe? It's like they knew we were coming!" We stayed there awhile and talked and laughed like "old friends" do. I remember sitting at that table thinking "I remember why I fell in love with you".

Yes as we looked back last night, your Aunt and I, . . . I said it was "AS IF" . . . "as if God knew somehow that HE was going to send you out with a little bit of special moments and time with those that you loved."

Your Aunt agreed but then suggested "what if it was as if God did it for THOSE OF US LEFT BEHIND?"

I hadn't really thought about that but you were just 2 months shy of being called home. We were just about to lose a man, husband, father, friend, nephew, and cousin who we loved so much. God did give us a gift in those few short days. This gift was a small window. We would find ourselves looking back through the panes of this window over and over again to see your smile, feel your touch, hear your laughter, to see that look of love in your eyes. We didn't know it then but God was laying the ground work for us, the grieving. HE knew what HIS plan was for you, but us, HE had to give us a way to keep going on without you, a way to remember you with a smile and not just a tear.

Isn't it funny . . . what we here on earth speculate to be "AS IF" . . . God is up there smiling saying, "No . . . it was really . . . AS PLANNED."

Always, ♥ djb

JULY 23:

Dear Dennis:

I sure did miss you this weekend. We had babies in the house and I couldn't help but wonder what it would have been like when we reached the age and we had "grand-babies" in the house. You loved little ones even though those teens made you a little crazy every now and then. (ha). I hope you are with me this week. Each day, each minute. Loving you always, ♥ djb

JULY 24:

Tomorrow before most of you have had your first cup of coffee I will be on my plane ride back to the "home land" ha. I will be heading back to hug and love on so many that I miss so much. This will do my heart good. Prayers are always welcome for safety, sweet memories and treasured moments for all. I will be taking my favorite angel with me (of course, as I go nowhere without him) and you all are going too . . . watch for the picture posts and you can share a little piece of home with me. Also, I just wanted to say that today has been a rough day for many (I have seen quite a few posts) but I haven't missed a one of you and keep each of you in my prayers and thoughts !!

JULY 30:

Dear Dennis:

Don't think for one second that I didn't miss you this weekend. I thought of you so much and wanted to call you and share all the details. So instead of dialing the phone I called God in prayer and ask him to share. There were some special moments that would have made you proud. I love you always and forever. ♥ djb

BUFFALO, NEW YORK . . . HOME SWEET . . . WAIT . . . I'M NOT FROM THERE . . .

We must have driven the eastern seaboard between Florida and New York hundreds of time. It all led to one place. Buffalo, N.Y. The birthplace of Dennis James Bujanowski, the love of my life. The temporary residence of Timothy and Sarah (my son and daughter) when they lived with their birth father. The home of many of Dennis' relatives who we love, the home to many relatives of the kids who we love and let's not forget the birthplace of the ever famous "Chicken Wing".

I am sure there were other things that Buffalo was known for besides the above and yes of course, "Lake Effect Snow", but for the reasons listed I became a "Buffalo Native by Default". I can't tell you how many times someone I worked with over the years in the Travel Agency said, "Oh Debra is from Buffalo, aren't you Debra? Tell them about Niagara Falls!" Ummmm, no I am actually from Three Rivers, Michigan—SW Michigan—where there really are three rivers (Rocky, Portage and St. Joe thank you!). Here, let me point to my hand and show you—Three Rivers is due south of Grand Rapids and Kalamazoo (Yes there really is a Kalamazoo).

I was not born in Buffalo, I did not go to school in Buffalo, I did not get married or divorced in Buffalo, I did not give birth in or to a Buffalo, I have never been a resident of Buffalo. There was this one time that Dennis tried to get me to eat buffalo and that left me feeling incredibly, shall we say, *disloyal to the homeland* yet somehow it was not "my" homeland.

I did however spend many wonderful nights in Buffalo, N. Y. and the surrounding area and I feel I know more about this great city than I do the one in which I claim as my birthplace. I am a die-hard Buffalo Bills fan (and if you are going to be a Bills fan you really need to go "all the way" and be "die-hard" because gosh darn it they ARE going to make a "comeback"). I do not care to hear about wide-rights or the number of Super Bowls they went to and didn't win. Nor do I want to debate anyone's opinion of the difference and level of greatness between quarterbacks, Jim Kelly and Doug (Oh my

God you are beautiful and I have actually met you once in person and still have your box of Flutie Flakes and autographs) Flutie.

I have watched the Buffalo Sabres hockey team for years and for this reason, I can sing the "Canadian National Anthem", know why there is a Timothy Horton's chain in N.Y. and LOVE their coffee, think Rick Jennerette's voice is the most amazing thing in sports broadcasting EVER, and do not wish to talk about the year the Sabres lost the "Stanley Cup" to the Dallas Stars (even if it was more than one).

I can make some seriously great "Chicken Wing Soup" which in its original state was created from scratch by a local Buffalo restaurant. I love Weber's mustard; believed for years that Anchor Bar hot sauce was just as important a condiment as ketchup, and felt some strange connection to NBC's Buffalo born Tim Russert, which caused many Buffalo natives tremendous sadness upon learning of his sudden death.

Last but not least I have seen the Niagara Falls from Canada, from the U.S., in the winter (Oh dear Gosh was that cold), in the spring (stunning), in the summer (it's so hot seriously you are just hoping you lose your footing, slip and go over), and most breathtakingly in the fall. I have seen the Falls from a plane (most amazing), by boat (Maid of the Mist), from the lookout deck, and while that is all pretty impressive . . . don't ya' know . . . I would like to be honest and say that the only two more famous ways you can see the Falls would be "on your honeymoon" and "going over them in a barrel", neither of which have I done (which is odd considering I have married THREE times to TWO men from Buffalo, ONE of which I was always looking for a way to get into that barrel.)

So there you have it . . . Buffalo Native by Default, like it or not, that is how it all played out. Truthfully, I liked it! A lot! It was Dennis, it was the kids at one point in their lives, it was his family, it was our sports teams, it was the food and the spirit and the attitude and the weather and it was just . . . Home Sweet Home! If you are from there you know the weather can be horrid. Sadly the economy is most times not great. The taxes are *h*igh, but the people are strong, amazing, hardworking, loyal to their town, their heritage, their sports teams, their city . . . If you are from Buffalo you are very proud to say you are from . . . Buffalo. One more key point . . . If you are from there . . . you . . . well . . . you sometimes sing about your food!

There is a fast food chain in Buffalo named Mighty Taco. Dennis LOVED Mighty Taco. If he could talk his Aunt or cousin into a late night run, while in town, all the better. As I mentioned in another chapter when we crossed the New York state line he would begin to sing, "Mighty Taco! Mighty Taco! Beef, bean, and cheese burrito with sour cream and jalepeno! Mighty Taco!" It was not quite as touching a moment as you may have envisioned but it was tradition none the less. Personally, I was loyal to the "other" famous taco chain and because Dennis knew that I did "all things Buffalo" out of my love for him but just could not bring myself to "sing the praises of this local cuisine" as it were, he let me off the hook and made the side trip to the "other guys" just for me whenever possible.

I used to think that singing about a taco fast food chain was just a little "wide-right" (did I say that?) but then I went to a Buffalo Bills vs. Jacksonville Jaguars game one year and directly behind me were four of the biggest, craziest, loudest, most obnoxious and incredibly funny Buffalo Bills fans you had ever seen in your life and what were they chanting? Oh yes they were! "Mighty Taco! Mighty Taco!"

So, while I am not from this great city, because of my sweet man and my children, I will always have a special place in my heart for Buffalo, N.Y.

Go Bills !!!

AUGUST 2012

(Facebook daily posts)

Marking Time

AUGUST 1:

It is with a good ♥ that my daughter did the following while I was gone. She was in Lowe's with her friend and saw an "OMG Mom he was so cute" man, bald ("but don't let that scare you Mom" because again OMG he is so cute), standing in the carpet section. She approached him and asked him if he was married. (Yes, I know). I feel it is at this point he may have been looking for cameras, Chris Jansen of NBC Dateline (To catch a Predator). He gave her a look and she said, "Oh no, it's not for me, it's for my Mom!" She went on to tell him that I had lost my husband and I that I was very pretty, cute and funny and then drilled this guy better than EHarmony ever thought about. This is what she learned from her 50 questions: His name is Brian, he is 47, he works as an electrician, he has 1 daughter 27, and 4 grandbabies. He likes dogs, hates cats, has a girl that he has been dating for 6 mos. but Sarah was sure to ask "are you in love" and he said, "no". She explained that her Mom needed a guy friend (at least in her mind I do), that I was very funny, and I would "cook for him" and she thought we would be in love if we met and told him I loved to talk but I was also a good listener "whatever he preferred". He likes alcohol, does not have a temper and she quizzed him on if he had a prison record (after she gave him my name and number). She said "if you have been arrested for rape or murder well then you are going to have to give back the number". Both Sarah and her friend said he was beyond cute, looks like some famous bald guy, has "wrinkles around his eyes" when he smiles and they were impressed how friendly he was and that he went along with this. He told them that he thought it was sweet that she was trying so hard for her Mom. Sarah told him that he could either call me today and talk to me OR if he didn't want to he could ask for Sarah and back out but either way he could not just NOT call. She was encouraged as he said, "So if I take your Mom out what would be a first good date?" Her only regret? "I didn't follow him into the parking lot to see what he drove Mom?" (Oh dear God !)—I WILL BE SURE TO POST IF MY PHONE RINGS !! (My first words to Brian . . . . I am so sorry my daughter accosted you in the hardware store Sir!

AUGUST 1:

Dear Dennis:

There is a country song called "Moments" by Emerson Drive that I have loved since the first time I heard it. It touches on something that I live for . . . "Moments". Moments in time that are just captured in your mind like a snapshot, burnt into your memory, stamped on your heart like a road map that leads from "where you come from" to "who you have become", moments that never leave you. When you hear of the elderly forgetting those they love standing in front of them but recalling something that happened 40, 50, even 60 years ago . . . it's "moments" that their hearts won't let their minds forget. Well this weekend Dennis, I had one.

I was attending my 30 year class reunion in Michigan. I was apprehensive about going home, flying, being on my first long distance trip without you, leaving the kids and the house, etc. I prayed on it, I talked about it and the excitement overtook me and I jumped on that plane and went. What happened was this . . . I was given an honorary mention at my reunion. I have been sharing my words, tears, grief, fear and love for a man like no other with whomever would listen. I never hide nor do I hesitate sharing you as you were my reason for everything, you were a man of no fear and a joy without end for us. I did not begin sharing all of this with others for any other reason than my heart was so deeply shattered that I couldn't breathe and writing was my only way it seemed to come up and gasp for air.

It seems that these words, this grief, all that was you and our love, have somehow helped others, lifted others, inspired others and possibly shown them that there is hope for the surviving souls. This is hope of the best kind. This is hope in knowing that you will smile again, laugh again, love again and breathe again without gasping when you do. I was so touched when they said these words about me, it seemed impossible because for these words to be spoken, what had to happen was I had to lose you. How incredible is that. So the irony is this my love. I honor you and for this they honor me . . . and I would trade it all in for just one more "moment" in your arms. I promised you when I said goodbye that day I would make you proud. While my tears were falling and these words were being said at this reunion, I was praying and thinking, "God Dennis how I hope you are with me right now and see this as that promise to you." I love you always, ♥ djb

AUGUST 4:

Dear Dennis:

I am having a hard time missing you these past few days. I am pretty sure it's because I picked up writing again and the memories will always do that to you, and Tim is leaving Tuesday and that is something that I would have heavily counted on you to carry me through. Sarah Jane is recovering from her first real broken ♥ and you and her were so close I know you would have helped her through this. Missing you sucks !! No really it does . . . so I will go back to what works, keep busy, exercise more, pray and get back to church. I am sure my house will be very clean at the end of all this missing you . . . so there's the plus side. Love you always, ♥ djb

AUGUST 4:

Just an observation. Lately I have talked to more than one person who has gone through divorce, breakup, loss through death, etc. What I keep hearing is "I don't care", "Never again", "I am done" . . . Amazing . . . did anyone get that each of these relationships all started with "OMG", "I want you, need you and love you", "You are my best friend."

I know this is a defense mechanism. There is NEVER a reason to give up on love my friends, never. My ♥ is certainly broken but I will love again, why, because the joy of loving will always outweigh the pain of losing.

AUGUST 4:

This is the note that was on my desk.

SARAH LOVES YOU ♥

REASONS:

You're me, but older

You're kinda funny I guess

You're pretty

You understand a lot

You're a Mom & Dad at the same time

You like to shop

You're not scared of anything (EXCEPT SNAKES—CHICKEN S&*T)

You're smart

You're coming now, finish later ♥

Sarah Jane

AUGUST 5:

Dear Dennis:

We are 30 days away from you being gone a year and I want you to know that I received an email from your former Manager asking how we were and if there was anything that the "team" could do for us. He talked of how much you were still missed every day. I am so proud of you baby . . . that speaks volumes to the man you were! Always, ♥ djb

AUGUST 7: (Timothy leaves for U.S. Army Basic Training)

Dear Dennis:

Please stay with our boy. I will be ok, but that is where I want you to be. Always, ♥ djb

AUGUST 7:

I said a year ago that I would NOT change my profile picture from Dennis until we had marked a year of his passing. In honor of my beautiful son taking the steps to manhood to protect and fight for our freedom, I will place Timothy's picture as my profile picture as of today (He is on his way to Columbia S.C. as we speak) and I will leave this up until he returns. I not only know that Dennis would understand, I know with all of my hear he is so incredibly proud of OUR son.

AUGUST 7:

Dear God:

May this pit in the bottom of my stomach not remain here until October. Not knowing if your child is ok is not ok. I can't imagine how you feel. I think my body is revolting as I have physically felt awful since he has left. I know I am not the first Mom and I wish there was a prayer that would allow me to be the last that feels this way when their son or daughter goes to basic or is deployed. It's just not ok. Please keep Timothy Beckwith and the rest of our babies as they take the steps necessary, as they do what so many others have done before them, as they answer a call that not everyone hears or can hear, as they become the men and women of our United States Military. I am missing my son already tonight and no words will change that. Please watch over my son. Amen.

AUGUST 8:

Dear Dennis:

Remember how you always called me an "odd bird" because I would eat "real food" for breakfast. I ate whatever was left over for dinner vs. breakfast food. You also remember how you took me out for sushi all the time and said you wouldn't stop until I loved it as much as you did This morning I had sushi for breakfast. just sayin' . . . I blame you !! Your odd bird loves you. Always, ♥ djb

AUGUST 9:

Dear Dennis:

I feel it safe to say that I haven't had a good night's sleep since you left. When you would take a business trip I would toss and turn at night until you came home. Then you would laugh at me because I couldn't wait to go to sleep when you got here. It's funny how you get used to sleeping with someone and the comfort it brings. Molson is still on my side of the bed on the floor, Mocha is still on your side, but now I still wake frequently throughout each night and think of you. Missing you always, ♥ djb

AUGUST 10:

Dear Dennis:

Anyone that knew you personally could hear you say your ever famous "it is what it is" response to most things that others found alarming or unsettling. I have mentioned this in a few of my stories of you. You rarely bought into the "drama" of it all and just had a "no fear and no BS" attitude about most things. This was the calming effect you had on our family. When the tears fell from my eyes because I am the hyper sensitive Mom, daughter, sister, friend who wears her heart on her sleeve . . . you always found a way to bring it back to what "it is" and assure me that simply breathing in and out was the answer. (Ok sometimes you said violence was the answer but we never really explored that further! ha) I miss the security of that calming effect. When I feel myself start to get stressed or react I just repeat your words in my head . . . "it is what it is". The reason I write this today is because as I was going through one of those catalogs that came with the "cool stuff" in it, in there was a stainless steel plate on a leather bracelet band carved with the words . . . "It is what it is". I am pretty sure it was meant to be that I see this and placed my order. Always, ♥ djb

AUGUST 19:

Dear Dennis:

I am sorry I haven't written in a while. So much going on here. Timothy in basic training has consumed my every thought, but you know I saved a few for you in my quiet moments. I hate Sunday mornings with rain and you not waking by my side. Tuesday our girl starts her senior year and I will be getting back into my routine of exercising since my travel is done. I am still writing of our love, time and silly moments and you are never far from my thoughts and heart. My prayer is that you are hanging at the Army base providing Timothy with comfort, courage and strength. Loving you always babe. ♥ djb

AUGUST 20:

Dennis and I banked at the same bank (quite naturally) and after he passed I of course canceled his accounts appropriately. While I was gone a new debit card came from the bank and I of course thought it was MINE with just an updated expiration date as it was a year longer validity than mine. So without looking I try to activate the card. It doesn't take, I try again, it doesn't take, I look at it carefully and it says DENNIS J BUJANOWSKI. Oh my gosh the tears came flooding so fast I didn't even have time to think. I wish things like that didn't throw me so quickly and so easily. I called the bank and straightened that out but it just hurts to be reminded so often that he's gone.

AUGUST 21: (SARAH JANE IS A SENIOR !!!)

Dear Sarah Jane:

Look both ways before you cross in front of the bus, don't share your drink with other kids, do not touch the boys they have cooties, place your right hand on your heart and DEMAND to say the Pledge of Allegiance, remember you are better than no one, and there is no one that could benefit more than by having you as a friend, manners are of the highest priority, if you can hear a teacher's voice they shouldn't be able to hear yours. Oh wait this is not K-Garden . . . you are on the edge of being a woman and an adult, lead by example, set the standard high, be a friend to many, and a blessing to all and honey ROCK YOUR SENIOR YEAR LIKE NO ONE EVER HAS !!! You are amazing because God and I made you that way, don't waste a minute of that. Happy 1st Day of School !! YOU ARE A SENIOR SARAH JANE !!!!!! OMG SISTER !!!

*** WE *** LOVE YOU, Mom & ♥ Dennis & Timothy & G-MA ! . . . ♥ mom

AUGUST 21:

Dear Dennis:

This morning I drove our girl to her 1st day of her Senior year. Last night she was missing you and how you would have been so excited for her and enjoyed sharing all of what this year will bring. I try to remember that it's not just me that misses you even though we all show it and deal with it in different ways. You are so imbedded in our hearts babe and your love for us will never be forgotten. If there is one thing I could teach my daughter about love it **would be** . . . nothing is more precious, nothing is more sacred between two hearts, and love should never be taken for granted !! Watch over our babies please . . . you always made us feel safe and they will forever nee**d you. Loving you always, ♥ djb**

AUGUST 24:

Dear Dennis:

It's 4 a.m. And again I am up with a headache. Too much on my mind, worrying about Tim (that won't go away no matter what), missing you and trying to figure out how to balance all that needs to get done. It is funny as if you ever got overwhelmed I would just reassure you that it would all be ok and pick up the slack somehow but doing this all without you can get a little much. God bless the single parent . . . whew! I am thinking of cloning myself but I can still hear my Dad say "thank God you weren't twins". I am sure if he knew the reason I needed two of me . . . he would approve. Ha. Well I will quit feeling sorry for myself, go make some coffee and tackle whatever today brings. I miss you so much. Just as much today as months ago. Always, ♥ djb

AUGUST 26:

Dear Dennis:

This is why you said you loved me remember? Because I would cry and be worried for a couple of days when things got to be too much, BUT I ALWAYS get up and stand tall against the forces that try to destroy good, happiness and love. Today, even though I miss you and Tim, even though I can feel a slight bit of worry, I will listen to all of my friends who have said, "Worrying changes nothing". I now have my coffee in hand, I am going to tear my office apart and rearrange it, work more on the book by doing some more writing and organizing of chapters, pray and write to my son . . . just one foot in front of the other. Life is just hard, it's just that simple but I have it better than so many others who are suffering so I will stop with the ME, and reach out to someone else whose need is greater than mine.

You? Dennis you stay with Tim, watch over him please. Never forget we pull much strength from you every day and love you endlessly !! Always, ♥ djb

AUGUST 28:

Dear Dennis:

I have been trying to channel you here lately. I know what you would say if I could speak to you right now and I am trying to remain calm and think how you would handle this. You would get angry and strong, I would get sensitive and logical, and then we would go with something in between! ha. When you are taking on EVIL you must wear a suit of armor and it must hold metals and fibers of intelligence, logic, strength, integrity, cleverness, love and faith. I won't lay this all on God, as he only helps those that help themselves and those that literally can't help themselves. Well, I fall into the first category and I am not going to let EVIL penetrate my armor. We built this suit of armor you and I, we decided it's color and the materials it should hold. I think you wore it more than I, but when you left I knew I would have to put it on one day without you. You can laugh but I think it's the "perfect size" and it looks great on me. Hang with me baby, this is all a part of the "make you proud" promise. Always, ♥ djb

AUGUST 31:

Dear Dennis:

It's Friday !! While that may not mean much in a place like heaven that does not mark time, here this is a significant day and day of the week. It's the end of the work week which is what you and I always lived for so we could enjoy our US time and family time. It is the last day of August 2012 and so begins the 25 day count to the 1 year of your passing at which point I will no longer be writing you in this format. It is the day that the U.S. Army posts new pictures of our soldiers in training and I will pray for a glimpse of our young man Timothy. It begins the 8 day count to our little girl Sarah's 17th birthday. I am not sure exactly yet how that happened. Every day is a gift here on earth, everyday could be our last and yet every day is recorded as "another moment in the days that make up the life of . . ." So while it may just be TGIF to some it goes way deeper than that on my calendar. I pray daily your soul is resting and instead of TGIF, I proclaim today and all other days . . . TGFY. Thank God For You. Always, ♥ djb

HE THINKS HE MARRIED
JODIE FOSTER

In October 2010, Dennis went into the hospital for an ablation. Ablation is a technique used to treat abnormal heart rhythms, or arrhythmias, and can be done surgically or non-surgically. Dennis had A-fib and he had been treated for it for some time but they just couldn't keep him "out" of A-fib and after other methods and medicines were tried this was determined the best plan of action.

I of course was worried sick as anyone would be when their loved one goes in for a surgical procedure. When I heard that they went in and burned areas in the heart muscle I just about became a nervous wreck praying that nothing would go terribly wrong. I kept tearing up and repeating "I love you" just before they took him back and he said again as he always did, "it is what it is Debra. I love you too and I will be just fine and *if I am not you know what to do*". It always seemed so easy as far as his understanding of how I would go on if he were no longer there. Maybe that was his faith in me and I didn't know it, maybe it was because he knew I would have no other choice.

They told me he would in the operating room for 1.5 hours and that I could wait in the designated waiting area. They said when they were done the Doctor would come out and speak to me personally to tell me how "it went". I went to the cafeteria on the next floor to get a cup of coffee and even though I was gone less than 15 minutes, I rushed to get back as "what if they come for me and I am not there?"

I brought my book, my phone, my crochet and anything to keep me busy and to keep my mind off of what was really happening. Of course, I can multi-task like any good woman so I was crocheting baby blankets while I was taking in all conversations around me, listening as the Doctor's would come and tell a family "how it went in there" and what to expect going forward. I waited, I read, I called my friend in Jacksonville and talked to her as I knew she would calm my nerves and make it "all okay". There was something else I did as I waited, and I did it more intently than I did anything else . . . I prayed silently and watched the clock.

When one and half-hours had passed, not a minute less, not a minute more I began my slide into apprehension. I knew Dennis would chastise me for this if he knew, and trust me he knew, but I was holding them to their word. Anything beyond the allotted time, anything outside of "standard operating procedure" as they had explained it to me would sound an alarm in my head and slowly begin the tightening of my heart muscle. What if something did go wrong? What if they came out and it wasn't okay? Really, I was just supposed to walk away with "It is what it is Debra"? I prayed silently "Dear God, let them come in here NOW, let him be okay."

It was approximately another 30 minutes when I called the nurse's station from the phone in the waiting room and was simply advised they "were almost finished." It was almost an hour beyond their allotted time when a Doctor stepped into the room and said, "Bujanowski." Unlike the other families that were approached right where they sat, this Doctor motioned to a small side room and proceeded that way assuming I was following. Oh I was I promise you, but God help me I was trembling the entire way. He asked me to sit down and I refused. I think all I got out of my mouth was "just tell me". Expecting the worst, he said Dennis had made it through okay but they had much more areas to burn or work on than they had originally expected. He provided me with the information that I needed to care for him going forward and stated that it was his hope this would keep him out of A-Fib. When tears of relief fell down my cheeks he touched my arm and said, "he is okay I promise". I was then advised that I could go back and see him as soon as the recovery nurse came out to get me.

I wiped my face, gathered my things and waited for another few minutes until the recovery nurse arrived. We walked down the hall together and she began to tell me that Dennis was okay but he was still much drugged and very groggy. She said, "What a sweet man, he was so worried about you." She continued with, "Really you are not supposed to be back here but he insisted and started to get agitated that you were not with him and that you were out here in the waiting room and were probably worried sick, he almost demanded that we come get you." That made me cry a little, bless his heart, he was always thinking of me even when I didn't give him credit for doing so. She saw my tears and she stopped walking just outside the Recovery Room doors. She said, "There is just one other thing I should probably mention" at which point she began to smile. When I asked her what it was she said, "Well, he did say all of those things I just told you and he did indicate that he was very worried about his "*wife*" but when I asked him what your name was so I could call you . . . well, . . . well . . . **he thinks he's married to Jodie Foster!**".

"He does? Does he?" was all I could get out between the tears and laughter. Oh my Lord, that man.

I guess I need to tell you that Dennis has had a very long crush on Ms. Foster. I admit I might have made a few tasteless jokes in the past regarding how it didn't compare to the other well-known crush that we all were aware of for this lovely actress. He would say, "there's my baby" whenever he saw her on TV. I never really "got it" but since I was the one who got to marry him, I was willing to let this "love" live its course.

I came through the door telling the nurse, "if he calls me Jodie ***I am pulling the plug***" which she greatly appreciated. He smiled a weak smile and I grabbed his hand. I said all of the things you would expect for this type of greeting and again I was told I only had just minutes to stay. I kissed his cheek, told him I loved him and asked how he felt. I stayed only a moment longer and just as I was turning to leave I said, "Dennis do you know who I am?" Talking was painful for him and I got another smile and nod. I said, "So, you are married to Jodie Foster hey?" At the sound of her name his grin became wider and I said, "Well that's great baby because my husband Jon Bon Jovi is just outside those doors and I must go now as he is waiting for me."

He promised me later that he had NO memory of telling the nurse that he was married to Jodie. That was October. Come December on Christmas Day I opened my gift from Dennis. It was a brand new large size Kindle. I was stunned and thrilled as you can imagine how much I loved to read and would enjoy this. I knew they made smaller less expensive versions but like all things "Dennis" it had to be the biggest and the best. Later that night as we were alone in our room, I told him how much I loved my gift and that he didn't have to buy me the bigger size but I appreciated it. He told me, "This year has been hard, and you never left my side, you were always there for me and you were such a good nurse when I was in the hospital recovering from my surgery. I just wanted to let you know how much I love you and appreciate what you did . . . (PAUSE) . . . ***Jodie***!".

WHAT'S IN A NAME?

Let's just get this out in the open right now shall we? I am not Elizabeth Taylor nor have I been married as many times as she, but each time I did marry (3) I had to make that wonderful decision of whether to keep my delicate birth/maiden name of BLOOD, or to take the name of the man I was about to enter holy matrimony with (again), said *Debra Jane Blood Lacey Blood Beckwith Blood Bujanowski Blood*

Growing up as a young girl, with a name like BLOOD, was truly an experience. I believe by the time I became a young woman in my 20's I had more nicknames than Heinz had pickles. To name a few . . . Blood, Plasma, Hemoglobin, Band Pants Blood, Bubba, Deb-a, De-BRA, Bloody, Reynolds (after movie actress Debbie Reynolds), Freckles, Brown-Eyes, Sweaty Nose (don't ask), Deeb-E, Deb J, Jane, Deb, D, D.J., Debbie, Derb and probably a few more that I am forgetting. When I moved away from Michigan to start a new life in Florida, I decided that starting over was indeed called for . . . therefore, I became Debra J. Blood, nice to meet you I am simply, Debra.

My family has this thing about initials and using the same first letter when naming siblings. There is Gary & Glenn, Julie, Jim & Jeff, Michele & Michael, Dave & Deb (that's me), Margaret & Martha . . . well you get it. I was born Debra Jane Blood, after my mother Ramona Jane Blood, and then I named my daughter Sarah Jane (Beckwith) so the R.J.B, D.J.B., and S.J.B. have been established and I have shown no dishonor to this silly family tradition and I am sure this allows me to be forgiven for naming one child Timothy and the other Sarah.

One of the first times I was in the same room with Dennis it was at his home in Jacksonville. I was sitting at his table listening to my brother David, Dennis and a few others rambling on as men will do (and they say us girls can talk?). I helped myself to a pen and a piece of paper that were lying on the table and I did what any bored woman would do, I doodled. As I wrote DJB—DJB—*DJB*—over and over and over, and then Debra J. Blood, *Debra Jane Blood* in cursive, in block, in bold, as a design, and proceeded to color it in . . . I soon became engaged in one of the first and most mature conversations that Dennis and I have ever had. It started with Dennis staring at my beautiful artwork and asking the obvious question (to him) . . . "Why are you writing *MY* initials over and over?" Without hesitation, I waived him off with a simple, yet adult response of "Ummmm they are *MY* initials and I am bored". To which he replied, "NO! They are *MY* initials" (because you know only one human can have the same initials in the world—that is a man rule apparently!). I said, "Well, this may come as a shock to you but I was born **D**ebra **J**ane **B**lood, and clearly they are mine!" Just as maturely, he said, "Well, I was born **D**ennis **J**ames **B**ujanowski and if you and I get married someday (getting a little ahead of ourselves are we there Dennis?) imagine how much money we will save on monogram towels?" (Eyes locked—grins engaged) Really Dennis? That's your sales pitch? Save money on towels? I left him with, "Well, I guess that's as good of a reason as any to get married, as every other one I have thought of, up to now, has been seriously a bad idea!" He left me with a silly grin and his ever famous, "Hmm?"

As it came to pass of course we did get married. I don't believe we ever had a lot of monogram towels so I can honestly say we "did save money" on that idea. However, the nickname cloud that hung over me as a young woman never really dissipated. Once I spent time with Dennis, I became affectionately known as "Debbie" whenever he wanted something or was begging for forgiveness or should the subject of MY COOKING ever come up. "Debbie you know I love you right?", "Debbie what are we having for dinner?", "Debbie, I am sorry I am late?", "That was a pretty good meal there Debbie !".

It didn't end there. Dennis loved nicknames. He loved to make up names and use them every chance he got. He did this with me, he did it with the kids, he did it with the dogs, and he did it with the cat. It was what he did, he loved it and we love him because of it. I am going to share some names with you and try to explain their origin and I hope you overlook what may seem inappropriate to younger viewers and appreciate the intended humor instead.

Debra—Nickname—Mama Big Boobs (I do not know why he called me this ! lol)

Debra—Nickname—Weiner Mom (This started with Timothy).

Dennis—Nickname—Weiner Dad (By default of course, everyone else got their names first)

Timothy—Nickname—Weiner Boy (Believe it or not Tim hated this name at the start but near the end he thought it was so funny that they were Weiner Boy and Weiner Dad, they even signed cards to each other this way).

Sarah—Nickname—Weiner Girl (Well? After all she was Weiner Boy's sister)

Timothy—Indian Nickname—Knocked on butt by black boy (which he literally was at a NFL event for kids.)

Sarah—Nickname—Pigeon Lip Pumpkin Bobber (I can't remember how this all came about but it was a family favorite for sure. I know it had something to do with her pouting and sticking her bottom lip out as a little one.)

Sarah—Nickname—Princess Rosa Corn (After her hair was put into little cute knots (by her Aunt) in "rows" that Dennis thought "looked like corn".)

Mocha—(Chocolate Lab) Nickname—Moo-ca, the Mocha, the Moooooooo (His baby girl !!)

Molson—(Black Lab) Nickname—Molson "the sky is falling" Blood (He was the nervous type !)

Shami—(Yellow Lab) Nickname—SUPER Shami (He loved to yell this loud and in an excited voice !)

Sarah—Nickname—SUPER Sarah (only because of Super Shami—said in the same way)

Cosmo—Nickname—Meow-zin-heimer.

Not only did he love nicknames, he also would hear a name or a commercial jingle that made him giggle and he would hang onto it for dear life.

There was a commercial about accepting differences in people. It showed a girl with down's syndrome winning the Homecoming Queen title and they would announce her name loud and clear, "Becca Weinager !!" . You could hear Dennis on any given day shout "Becca Weinager !!!" Why? We don't know but it made him giggle and us too.

He picked up the name "Mr. Barky Von Schnauzer" off of a commercial and we spent months hearing that repeated over and over as that just tickled him so much.

He would yell for no apparent reason . . . . GOOD MOOD FOOD!! (Arby's commercial).

When a boy would call the house to talk to Sarah (and he thought he was too old or wrong for her—that would have been ALL of them by the way) he changed the name on the caller I.D. to read, "Hell No". (I will spare you what the I.D. said when my ex-husband called ! Oh my . . .)

Years ago an insurance agent called our house and gave us all sorts of trouble with what we were trying to accomplish with our homeowners insurance. He was rude, he was not helpful at all and he seriously was not interested in keeping our business. It had all been decided that we were no longer doing business with this man or his company but unfortunately for him he called us "one last time" to try to "work it out". His name was Tom Bologna (that's right . . . my bologna has a first name . . . it's . . .). Dennis answered the phone that day and all I heard was, "Tom? Tom Bologna? Tom Bologna is it? Well I think you are full of BOLOGNA . . . TOM!!! I think I want to sing a good-bye song to you Tom! My Bologna has a first name . . ." Oh my goodness honey hang up the phone.

Dennis requested to "take my last name" of Blood, the day we applied for our marriage license. The nice lady said "Sir she can take your name of Bujanowski, by stating so right now, but for you to take her name of Blood, you will have to see a Judge." Well, now that's "discrimination" or so he explained to her as he tried to persuade her to waive the visit to the Judge with his sad saga of "Do you know how hard it is to order pizza?" or "Do you know what it's like to have them butcher your name at the Doctor's office waiting room in front of all of those people?" "Do you understand what it's like to never have your name spelled correctly? ", "Do you know how many polish jokes I have had to hear just because people see SKI on the end of my name?" . . . . "Do you? Do you know? Do you?" No Dennis, she didn't know, her name was SMITH, she didn't get it sweetie !!! While I feel she sympathized with his plight I am almost certain her sympathy was more with me as I signed that application for marriage.

So while I felt that I had personally made one too many trips to the Social Security office, and on any given day I could answer to any given name, I was never more proud or happier than to be called Mrs. Bujanowski.

CAN WE JUST AGREE THAT I AM ALWAYS RIGHT?

There is something incredibly annoying to me about people who have to "always" be right. I don't feel I am that way but then again I could be wrong, and yet I doubt it. (Queue laughter track) I don't feel that Dennis was that way. I do believe we held a nice balance between we agreed on most things and then it was very:

You were an ass on Thursday.

Which Thursday?

Pick one.

Where there is love, there is passion and where there is passion there is . . . fire.

I, Debra Jane Blood am here to tell you that Dennis James Bujanowski and I had many battles of will, mind, and space. Oh yes we did. Don't all married couples argue over small things, silly things that don't really matter?

It starts slowly with you trying to maintain your independence as a young married couple. You don't want to give in, give up, or let go and as time goes on you learn that what you are holding on to doesn't matter nearly as much as what you could hold everyday if you just said "I am sorry, I was wrong" more often. Words spoken in anger cannot be taken back and time spent not speaking over who was right and who was wrong is time you can never get back. Hard lessons learned.

He was strong in his personality. So was I. He was smart and determined. So was I. He had made his own way and earned everything that he owned by working hard every day. So did I. He was very proud of himself for doing so, as he should have been, so having someone else telling him the "way it was" was not going to fly on most given days. I was raised by a man who taught me exactly how to do just that. Stand up for yourself, defend what is right, speak your mind, and don't back down.

So what attracted us to each other was the very thing that caused many shaky moments in our marriage. Why am I sharing this? Because you can't get the roses without the thorns, isn't that what they say? I have said it so many times, "We were not perfect, we were just perfect together" and sometimes that means . . . the "perfect storm".

He always knew what to do, how to get it done, in what time frame, what manner and what strength was needed to make "it" happen. He would hit things head-on, full force and without hesitation. This all goes back to our core differences of "Debra wants to teach the world to sing" and "Dennis lived and died by an eye for an eye" and as he would say, "God help the man that messes with my family or my wallet."

There are serious issues that come into every marriage. We were a combined family. I had an ex-husband that was nothing short of "incredible" and I don't mean in any good way. I won't give him any credit here as that would only make him smile but for years the struggles over divorce, custody, Dennis raising step-children while being under minded by the ex and all that entailed consumed our lives. What we went through however *only brought us closer and strengthened our love and resolve* (Dear Ex-Husband if you are reading this . . . take note), but it did not come without tears, raised voices, sleepless nights and too many mornings of, "Ok I am sorry, I was wrong for saying that." It's just life. We all know it. We all live it. Some have it easier than others do and how you handle your differences can make or break any marriage.

One of the most common arguments that we had was over my seriously poor "sense of direction". I could not read a map to 'find my way out of a paper sack" as my love would so easily say. I saw a sign that said "I-85" and would turn at the very next road that came up thinking "Why else would they have mentioned it just then if that was not how to get to I-85?" I could make Dennis crazy enough to require the men in white suits to come just by trying to "navigate" as he drove. He would say, "Babe pull out the map, find where we are and tell me what the next exit is that has gas, food, etc." This was me, "Ok, that sounds easy and I am all about helping but um honey can we just go back to the part where I need to *find where we are* for a moment?"

Oh dear God, there was a trip to Baltimore that almost ended our marriage because of major roads missed. I think where he stopped to call a divorce attorney was somewhere around the third trip through the city after I tried to lighten the moment with, "Baby as long as we are together does it really matter exactly where we are?" (P.S. That didn't end well.)

He said when they invented GPS, "it's a good thing you can cook and I love you". Ah, the love—can you feel it?

Oh we fought over space in the closet, space taken up for my crafts or his tools. Then there was the *big stuff*, like . . . **Why** we had so many condiments in the refrigerator? God help us if there was more than two of the same item opened. He could not stand waste. He didn't understand why I didn't understand what I didn't understand. I understood alright, but what he didn't understand was what I had listed at the top of my "choose your battles" list was not even close to what he had on his list. We just didn't see the same things as a "big deal" so when one puts their priority where another does not, you will have conflict. He hated my driving and said "you should not be allowed on any interstate where the speed limit is over 50 mph." I did not like his driving and how he chose to "Earnhardt" someone when they got in his way. Why am I able to crochet now like a pro? Because it is what I took up to not have to watch the road and lose my mind on all those trips that he drove between Florida and Buffalo. Thank you Mr. Earnhardt!

I always ordered him fries with his burger. He HATED fries. "Why can you not remember that I hate fries Debra?" "Because the rest of the world knows you can't have a burger without them, the rest of the world eats fries, that's why every burger place in the history of burger places makes them the side order, just suck it up and eat the damn fries Dennis." Would it have been so hard to not order the fries? Probably not. Did I ever take that route? Never.

What is the root of all evil? Money. Exactly. Dennis was excellent with money. His father was amazing with the stock market and his mother worked doing other's taxes every year. He came by this naturally and we called him Mr. Math Man for this very reason. I was hopelessly horrible with keeping a checkbook. This made him insane. I would buy something "on sale" and he would not understand why it mattered if it was on sale or not if I didn't need it. It was the ridiculous little things that all married couples argue about.

We actually had an argument at the dinner table one night over God knows what in which I lost my temper and called him a not so nice name. I started it with me using the "A-hole" (Please tell me you haven't heard or said worse) name to which he responded with "face-hole" (hmmm, there's a new one) and these names were volleyed back and forth until he said the most "mature" thing I have ever heard him say . . . . "double face-hole". At that point we stopped, stared at each other with the look that said he had internally tallied the scorecard heavier on his side, and then we lost it completely laughing. Well, hey if you are going to argue like kids, you might as well do it up right.

So we were different yet very much alike. We were both so head-strong. We both had tempers. We both thought we had all the answers but on any given day we could and would argue about the questions. I respected Dennis for so much and while I don't miss any of the disagreements or bad times we had, I have come to understand that "being the softer side of Dennis" was what he thought me to be and I was very "okay" with this. I could argue matters of the heart and win hands down on any day of the week but if logic and rules were to decide the outcome . . . he declared victory.

Does your spouse snore? Okay mine did, like a freight train coming. He did this every night and it almost always ended with me gently poking him to wake him just enough to make it stop. Then came the angry "Why did you wake me?" followed by "Because you were snoring", followed by "No I was not" followed by me heading for the couch and then him being upset because I left our bed. When he tried to pull the "You snore too Debra" on me I always argued, "And when exactly are you awake enough to hear this while you are sawing logs?" I used to tell him I was sure I was not snoring because to snore you had to be asleep and I was not asleep, this I know, as I was certain I was awake plotting how I was going to use the pillow in some fashion to reduce the logs he sawed.

There can't be a person who is reading this who hasn't been there. No relationship comes without the ups and downs, struggles, fights for territory or independence. I learned over the years if I wanted something or I wanted him to see it my way, I had to play my cards at the right time and "bluffing" was not always a bad skill. I didn't "play him" but when I won him over with "feelings" he would just roll his eyes, shrug his shoulders and remind me that he fell in love with me because of my "big heart" and he accepted this for a part of who I was.

How many of you know NOT to ever do a home improvement project with the person that you love the most in life? Oh we knew it too I promise you, but we did it anyway. "No Dennis I don't know what kind of wrench that is." . . . "No Debra I am not going to go back and paint that spot one more time because you think the shading is wrong!" . . . "Ok, Dennis don't listen to me, you **are** doing it correctly, but when you are done cutting that piece of wood at the wrong angle and it requires another trip to Home Depot, I AM NOT GOING !!!" I am still amazed that we actually lived through the "re-siding of Treemont St." our first home in Jacksonville, FL without calling for medical, fire or police assistance.

It was never ending, but no one died, no one got hurt and most projects were pretty darn amazing when we finished. We always laughed and forgot whatever it was that we disagreed upon as soon as the pride in our accomplishments of what we did "together" took over.

Do I have regrets? Of course I do. Do I wish I could have shut up more, given in more often, argued less, and chosen my battles more effectively? God yes. Don't we all? But through it all, I know in my heart of hearts he knew that I respected no one more than him. He knew that I thought he was the smartest man I had ever known. But as I reminded him so many times . . . "If I didn't maintain MY point of view, I would lose myself and without ME, who would WE be?" He said that was "Debra logic". Maybe so, but it made perfect sense to me (i.e. Debra).

There were nights on the couch for both of us because we were too angry to NOT go to bed mad with each other. There were trips taken in silence, cold stares and tears shed for reasons I can't remember. We had our moments like the rest of the couples that said, "for good and for bad". We swore from the beginning that divorce was not an option and when really mad I am sure I said, "Ok but that only leaves one other solution!" (No I didn't mean it!)

I remember one night we got into a seriously huge argument over something ridiculous. I ended up on the couch and he in our bedroom. He came out to get something from the kitchen and on his way through the living room he made a half-hearted attempt to "break the ice". He said light heartedly, "Whatcha watching there *Debbie?*" To which I replied, "An episode of **Snapped,** care to join me?" . . . "Taking notes?" was all I heard him say as he went down the hall. That was us.

Since Dennis has died and I have been faced with making all the decisions, when I come across one that would normally fall into "his territory" you could hear Sarah say, "What do you think Dennis would think of you doing that?" It was with love in my heart for this man that I would always respond with, "If he wanted a say in the matter he wouldn't have died and left it up to me!"

Tasteless humor? Maybe but since I haven't heard him argue the point, I am going to assume I won that one!

I HAVE BEEN THERE

Yesterday I had went to a pain management clinic for my chronic back pain. Of course part of the process is to take blood and rule out various other things. I was sent over to the hospital to get this drawn. When I got there I was told to "go down that hall, through that door and speak to the lady at the desk just inside the door." This I did.

Lack of sleep and constant pain, as you know, wears on you. I was not really focused so to speak as I sat down in that chair but almost immediately I felt, "I have been here before". I couldn't get my mind around why this was so familiar but as the nice clerk took my papers and started to type, I scanned the area. She said, "Ma'am are you ok?" I kind of shook myself out of my stupor and replied with a dazed, "What?" She said, "Are you ok? You don't look so good." By the time the next words came out of her mouth, it hit me. Yes I had been here before. I had been in this room; I sat in the chair next to the one I was currently in. He sat in this one that holds me now. He sat here and gave his social and address. He was here to get blood work for his upcoming surgery for his heart. It had been nearly two years since I came to this place.

She read my name off of my paperwork and then said, "Have **you** been here before?" Funny you ask. It was then the tears came. I fought them back the best I could to no avail and said, "Well, yes, but you won't find me in your computer." I apologized and said, "I am sorry. The last time I was here I was with my husband, and he has since passed and being here is making me **have a moment**." She stopped what she was doing, reached over the keyboard, took my hand and quietly said, "God please ease his sweet woman's pain and let her husband know she still carries him in her heart." As you can only imagine . . . yes more tears.

I felt embarrassed and so upset with myself that I can't control these feelings or this onslaught of tears in public at times. I pass people every day in my travels and I search their faces and wonder . . . "Do you know how this feels?" and wonder "Have they lost someone too?" Grief is a gripping, elusive thing that can just sneak up on you anywhere, anytime, no notice, no warning . . . no mercy. Here I am going on two years later and it's still searching me out.

I did what I had to do. I dried my tears and headed to the car. As I made it to the car the tears were coming again, I said, "Jesus, Dennis could you help me out here and just make it stop?"

I left the parking lot and turned right. I came to the stop light. On my right, on the corner of the intersection was something also familiar. It is the "Community Garden". This is a fenced in area that volunteers have planted fruits and vegetables and maintained. They use the harvest to feed those in need. I have been at this intersection so many times. Each day I came to see him during his hospital stay, each procedure. As I looked at this small garden a smile came to my face. Then through the tears the laughter took over . . . and all I could hear was, "Thank God *you* didn't volunteer and those people were counting on you to feed them!" He was in pain and had just been released from the hospital and it was October 2010. Even though every breath and movement hurt him, he held his stomach as he laughed over his funny little joke of what was a "thumb—never to be green." I remember telling him that day, "Be nice funny man because you too count on me for nourishment you know!"

For every tear soaked memory, I have a laughter filled moment to cancel out the heartbreak. Grief knows no boundaries. Grief does not play nice or fair, and it most certainly does not know when it has "over stayed it's welcome." When your heart heals and the cracks are sealed, grief no longer has a place to reside. Grief may sneak up on me, it may overtake me momentarily but as it does I have a million pieces of time so sweet, so love filled, so cherished. These pieces make up a shield that I used to fight this horrible emotion and cause it to run back where it belongs . . . to my yesterdays.

THERE WAS THIS DAY . . . .
THIS MOMENT

There was this day . . . this moment . . . it still lives in my memory. You, me, laughter, smiles, unspoken words, a glance between us that spoke more than any paragraph of a new book I just couldn't put down. Breakfast at dawn. You said those were the "best eggs" I ever made. Coffee on the porch in rocking chairs. Water rushing loudly in the river below. Book stores, ice cream home-made, antiques, fishing tackle that you said will guarantee they bite. Unscheduled naps. Holding hands and walking slow. You cast a line, I read a page. You stand in the cold running water; I sit nearby on a large rock. Your joy is found in peace, my joy is found beside you. You start a sentence I finish it. I can't hear the phone ringing. The clock has stopped ticking. Nothing is counting time. Time more precious than gold.

There was this day . . . this moment . . . it still lives in my memory. They were so young. We slowed as they climbed from the back seat to "break the law" for only a moment. One by one they took their turn on your lap where you laughed, giggled, sang words that only you both could write. You in their world, them soaking in all that was yours. They felt your arms around them, safety, security and love absorbed from your body to theirs. Somewhere in their hearts you could hear the shutter of every snapshot being captured.

There was this day . . . this moment . . . it still lives in my memory. You said, "Sit down, we need to talk." They said it was not so bad, with medicine and care you would be fine. No reason for fear darlin' is what I think you said as you wiped my tears. I don't know as I can't hear words anymore. I know you are talking and I feel it was something about your heart but I can't be certain as it was mine that stopped that very day, that very moment.

There was this day . . . this moment . . . it still lives in my memory. We barely knew each other. We had time to share before the sun came up. Just a casual conversation held between new friends. You were a mystery. I was something you had not discovered before. You said you were looking for "her" . . . "the one". She must be kind, warm and full of love, have pretty eyes and smile, professional and nurturing. I said "he" must be strong, filled with honor and loyalty, determined, educated, affectionate and full of laughter. Hours passed. Stories shared. Dreams revealed with the sunrise. How were we to know then that a seed had been planted and our love began growing, truly on that day . . . at that moment.

There was this day . . . this moment . . . it still lives in my memory. Just home. It has been a long day. He wanted to shoot just a few hoops with you before you went in. You were so tired but . . . the look in his eyes. You were feeling younger than you knew. Just a few minutes, it won't take long. One jump. You came down hard. Your ankle gave way, inside you came limping to the couch. Call the doctor we offered. No get the Jack Daniels and some ice you said. Directions were given: One we could put on your ankle, one we could not.

There was this day . . . this moment . . . it still lives in my memory. The doctor said the surgery would cause "hot flashes" like I was an older woman. You said the black laced dress you bought me would be beautiful for a "young woman" to wear on our first real night out after my ordeal. You waited hours as I paid attention to every detail to be someone you could be proud to have on your arm as I met your co-workers for the first time. The "flash" hit me at the front door as we prepared to leave. My dress that you picked out just for me, soaked with sweat and tears . . . you said, "We have a hair dryer and a clothes dryer right? So we start over and you will be back to dry & beautiful instead of wet & beautiful in no time at all". I never felt more special than on that day . . . at that moment.

There was this day . . . this moment . . . it still lives in my memory. The roads were covered in snow and ice. We are almost there, it won't be long and we will be hugging our babies again. Turn here you said, no wait don't, too late, off the road the van spins around and around and careens out of control. Screaming your name the entire way we land softly in a big pile of snow. I punched your arm and said, please be more decisive the next time. We laughed. We hold each other for a long moment. The moment knows how close we came.

There was this day . . . this moment . . . it still lives in my memory. Pumpkin pie was baking in the oven for tomorrow we give thanks. I don't expect you until tomorrow but today the knock on the door came so late. As I answered the door you said just so clearly, so decisively, so blatantly, "I love you, I know I do and I don't ever want to be without you" . . . there was a 20 second pause and then . . . "Is that pumpkin pie you are baking? YOU BAKE? Oh my God, I totally love you!" No one else but you filled my heart on that day . . . at that moment.

There was this day . . . this moment . . . it still lives in my memory. You said you were not walking around the entire Daytona 500 racetrack just to get to the other side. There was this hole in the fence big enough for us all, I follow rules, you follow your head and heart . . . you did not come with a road map. Under the fence we went. I thought you were crazy. ***How could I*** *ever make it with a man who thought so differently than I did?* You were living on an edge. My residence had always been just a few inches from the edge for fear of going over. I experienced your world, your freedom, your love of life and how deeply you strived to feel everything to the fullest extent you could. ***How could I?*** . . . was no longer the question at that moment. ***How could I not?***

There was this day . . . this moment . . . it still lives in my memory. I never knew I could experience and feel another's heartbreak as I did the day I told you your Mother was gone. You shed a billion tears from take-off to landing but as the plane touched down there was this change. You said you felt God. He was with you, so was your Mom. You didn't cry another tear. You stood so tall, so strong. You did all that needed to be done. Love, pride and heartache flooded every sense I had. ***You honored her memory that very day at that very moment.***

There was this day . . . this moment . . . it still lives in my memory. You kissed me so sweetly and said, "I will see you at the altar". I woke to two dozen yellow roses and a note that said, "Today I marry my best friend." I became your wife, you my husband. Until death do us part we said. God was there, he wrote our vows. He was there, that very day, that very moment.

There was this day . . . this moment . . . it still lives in my memory. Everything is a fog, I can hear voices but I don't know what they are saying. My surgery must be over but the pain has not ceased. They told you only feed her soft foods, small portions. They would provide water and applesauce only they said. Where did you go? I open my eyes slowly only wanting to see you, but what is that? 10-15 small cups filled with pudding, jello and assorted fruits line my bedside table, surrounding a sweet yet simple bouquet of flowers. You appear with a smile showing so much love and pride at your grocery selections made out of your concern for me. It was with this small gesture that I knew I was forever safe and protected in your arms for each future day . . . each future moment.

There was this day . . . this moment . . . it still lives in my memory. He walked across the stage. They shook his hand and handed him his diploma. We stood and cheered his name. We were so proud. We finally could see all that we had worked so hard for but why can't I see you? Where are you? It is such an important . . . wait isn't the tie he has on one of your favorites? He picked it out that morning without knowing why it was so special, only that it was yours. All he said was he wanted you to be a part of this day . . . this moment.

SEPTEMBER 2012

(Facebook daily posts)

One Year Without You

SEPTEMBER 7:

Dear Dennis:

I have given much thought to "what I will do on 9/25/2012". I first thought how I was certain I would be a bucket of tears realizing you had been gone for a year and "now what?" I then thought, "He hated when I was a bucket of tears" because you never really knew what to do with me other than hug me and try to make me smile. When the kids lived in Buffalo for all of those years with their Dad, how many times did we say good-bye and how many times did I melt into that bucket? What did you always do? IMMEDIATELY, hugged me, kissed me, and said while taking my hand, "Come on . . . get in the truck!" We always ended up at a restaurant where you KNEW I wouldn't cry in PUBLIC, and by the time we were done eating my emotions were under control and you had me smiling again over something silly. God knows how protective you were over my heart. ♥ I will love you forever for that. Well, now I am using your wise ways to heal what you are not here to heal. I will take Sarah and Mom on 9/25/2012, we will go to Red Lobster, I will order a Canadian beer (If I can get it), Grilled Lobster and Scallops (your favorite) and a steak. We will have a toast to the greatest love of my life and a man who was loved by so many and a blessing to all that knew him. Always, ♥ djb

SEPTEMBER 10:

Dear Dennis:

I walked outside to get the mail today and it hit me. The smell of fall in the air. That's all it took and while leaves were falling around me, tears were falling on me. It's ok honey, it won't always be this way but sometimes things "assault your senses" without warning and you can't control the outcome of emotions. This was our time. This was what we worked hard all year long for so we could take this US time. You would always be so excited to gather your tackle and poles, and I would load up the books and crafts. We would spend our time together in solitude enjoying those things that made us relax but yet we could do just feet apart from each other. Now this time of year brings your passing to mind, but I will never see the colors change, feel the crisp in the air, nor smell the fall that I don't think of you or us or our time. Thank you for the sweetest seasons of my life. Always, ♥ djb

SEPTEMBER 15:

Dear Dennis:

Time is passing so quickly I almost can't keep track. Tim is mid-stream in basic training and just the other day I was fretting over him leaving. I miss you so much and just want nothing more to sit next to you and be able to touch your face, hold your hand and just talk to you again. I need to hear your voice. But these things are not possible. I wish others who take their spouses for granted and get aggravated with them so easy would try to look for the good or remember why they loved the other in the first place more often, as time is so limited.

God has brought me to another person who knows this loss and we talk, cry and laugh together over the reality of it all. I told her that when I talk to other Army Mom's we try to ask our sons to find each other and introduce themselves to each other so they have friends. No Mom wants their child to be alone.

It made me think that I almost wish I could pray that for you, so you could go meet her son and you could be together as friends up there as we are down here. Maybe you could serve as a tour guide of sorts for the new arrivals; you always were all about exploring every part of a new area, your GPS and silly maps. Just an easier way for us down here to picture you there and not hurt so much, as no wife wants their husband to be alone.

My prayer is that when my journey ends I will sit next to you and be able to touch your face, hold your hand and just talk to you again. My prayer is that I will hear your voice and you will start with . . . "I've been waiting for you babe, let me show you around . . ."

Always, ♥ djb

SEPTEMBER 17:

Dear Dennis:

It's been awhile since I have written. Do you hear me speak your name in the quiet of the day? It's just a nudge to let you know that I still ♥ you and think of you often. You are in my daily prayers and thoughts—no amount of time or distance will change that. I love you. Always, ♥ djb

SEPTEMBER 19:

Dear Dennis:

I was reading my old calendar pages and this time last year you and I had lunch together just down the road, as you took a break during your work day. I can't help but say or think, "Had we known" but there is no point in that now. I still have a note you left me that says, "Get to work pumpkin head. See you tonight in the love nest!"

Your affectionate way of saying "home". Gosh I miss you and your silly ways. I even miss you and your ornery ways. I am finishing up my book about our life together and while it makes me cry it also makes me laugh OUT LOUD VERY HARD at times. But my goal is that it will do this for anyone who reads it whether they know us or not. There were moments when we were just a comedy routine waiting to happen, and there were moments that were so hard that it had to be the hand of God that pulled us through it together. You came with such funny memories and moments and I am not even telling them all. I remember you each day for the man you were, the friend I had, the love I lost, the father who signed up to be . . . I remember you today with so much love in my heart. Missing you. Always, ♥ djb

SEPTEMBER 25, 2012

Our final good-bye

If you have trouble seeing God in the smallest of moments, if you doubt you have influenced others, if you think that your children aren't watching or listening let me help you understand by reminding you that this book started with a correlation between how my mother handled the loss of my father and then how I took her example and used it to make my way in the days following Dennis' death. The irony lives on in the words that follow.

It is by the grace of God that our most beautiful daughter Sarah Jane (17 years old) has walked tall this year, and while having her moments, she stood by my side, held my hand, made me laugh when no one could and cried right along with me. I love you Sarah and thank God for letting me be your Mother (even on the bad days). Dennis loved her so much and had such dreams for her future. They fought like cats and dogs on any given day but the bond between them was stronger than any one I have seen between a Step-Father and Step-daughter.

I posted my *last* "Dear Dennis" on Sunday, 9/25/2012 and while this is painful to read, it was only after I posted my last that I discovered that Sarah had posted her *first* "Dear Dennis" on the same morning. It did something for me and to me that I can't explain. Maybe as you read these words yourself there won't really be a need for that explanation.

My final "Dear Dennis" post-1 year anniversary of his passing

Dear Dennis:

One year ago today, I walked down a sidewalk to find that my life had forever changed in a blink of an eye. What I thought I knew, what I believed, what I held dear completely changed in that very moment. You were gone. If I were asked by a stranger today how I walked through the days following 9/25/2011, I would only be able to say "with my unshakeable faith in ONE and the resounding love of MANY." Time is an amazing thing . . . for I don't miss you any less today than I did a year ago. I still cry when I think of things you have missed, I still laugh when I remember something silly you said or did, I still wonder what you would be doing today had it been me to leave and I pray every day to make you proud as was my last promise to you.

If I could bring you back today I would, but then you would find a whole different person here waiting for you. I know in my heart if you had the choice to leave heaven you would not go, but if you did what would you think of this Debra? Would you admire the effort we have all made in living through this first year without you here? Would you know that just because we did move forward doesn't mean we left you behind? (Would you make me repaint the bedroom?? LOL) We carry you with us each minute of the day. It amazes me the things the kids say and talk about that have you written into each line. Debra, Timothy and Sarah will forever be better for having known and loved a man named Dennis.

I don't know where the next year or the one after that will take me but I do know that they will bring me closer to God and ultimately back to your arms again. I feel I have a lot of living left to do. But I also know I will never ever as long as I breathe stop loving you or thanking God for the time that was ours.

For a year I have kept your picture on my profile. To remember you, to honor you, to let the world (or my part of it) know what a great, sweet, strong, funny, intelligent, loving man you were. Now I know it was all a part of letting go. It was all a part of becoming Debra without Dennis.

Today with your blessing I will be taking down your picture as a symbol of going forward. The thought of going forward used to nearly stop me in my tracks, but I now know that I will move into each new day with that same picture of you right here in my heart.

God had HIS plan for me already laid out. It was HIS plan that you and I share a love in our time on earth. It was HIS plan that our time ended while our love continued on through our children, their future and our stories that called to be told. I couldn't imagine the days ahead if I tried.

I promise you that while I pray that I will love again (the greatest of these is love . . . Corinthians 13:13), I know there will never be a love that touches my heart or soul in the way yours did and to the depths that you have reached.

Rest in peace sweetheart until we meet again.

Forever yours,

Debra

Sarah's first "Dear Dennis" post-1 year anniversary of his passing

Dear Dennis:

Today is one year. One hell of a year. One year since I've seen your face, since I've heard your voice. Today is one entire year and I don't know what I'm supposed to do about that. Today everyone at school will be going on with their lives like it's just another day. Today no one will know how I feel, will understand that everything I do, everything I say will be consumed in thoughts of you. I remember it like it was yesterday. I remember Mom coming in the house and screaming my name. I remember unloading the dishwasher. I remember being frustrated that she yelled my name instead of just saying it calmly. I remember having an attitude when I answered, but I didn't know.

I remember what the front yard looked like. I remember what you were wearing. I remember her screaming "call 911 Dennis had a heart attack." I remember going numb. I remember feeling nothing. I remember wondering why I wasn't as panicked as I should have been. I remember being pissed at you that morning. I remember walking out on the side walk and seeing you laying there lifeless under that tree. I remember texting Katlyn, Angus, and Cody on the way to the hospital . . . and I remember seeing you on that hospital bed changing color because it was too late. I remember every word Mom screamed. I remember her crying, her begging you to wake up. I remember silently screaming WAKE UP but you weren't ever going to wake up again. I remember staying numb for weeks, crying for a minute, then stopping. I remember Tim hugging me at the hospital. I remember the lady asking Mom questions and me being pissed thinking, now obviously ISN'T a good time. I remember trying to turn it into a joke because I couldn't think of anything else.

I remember it taking a really long time for me to miss you. I remember being frustrated with Tim because he wasn't reacting how I thought he should have been though I'm sure I wasn't reacting perfectly either. I wish I knew if you could hear me when I talk to you. I wish I knew if you're with me when I need you. I wish I knew if you know how much I miss you. You've missed so many things this year it's unreal. I don't miss how angry we all used to be but do miss how happy we used to be. I miss our good days. I miss telling you a joke. I miss you being the only one who thought my jokes were funny. I miss going to you when I couldn't go to Mom. I miss you being on my side in arguments with Mom or Tim. I miss you giving me advice. I miss you telling me stories. I miss having a Dad when my other one sucked. I miss complaining about you. I miss you so much you'll never know.

I hope you know that no matter where you are, if you're even anywhere, I still love you. It's an entire year later and nothing has changed, except that I only miss you more than I did. I'm so sorry for never telling you that I love you. I'm sorry for not being a good daughter. I'm sorry for making you so angry all the time. But you've got to know, that I've been trying in small ways to make up for it in the last 365 days.

Today is going to reset the mark back to day one. The clock is going to start over and it's going to be the start of ANOTHER year without you, again. I don't know how I'm going to get through this but I guess in some way I'll learn. I'm going to have to go through a lot of things that I think I wouldn't have to if you were still here and it just sucks. I wish so bad to talk to you and hug you and smell your cologne, but not from the bottle. I wish so bad to see you smile again and hear you talk and laugh and feel happiness. This last year has been so hard. So full of anger, so full of bitterness, so much sadness and heaviness that no one really knows how to handle. Talking about it won't bring you back, crying about it won't bring you back, being angry at everyone around me, WON'T bring you back. So like I said, I just don't know what to do. I love you Dennis, I miss you, and I'll see you again.

Until next time, Sarah ♥

—

Precious posting from our son Timothy that called to be included in this book:

OCTOBER 18, 2012: OUR SON TIMOTHY'S POST ON HIS U.S. ARMY BASIC TRAINING GRADUATION DAY, HILTON FIELD, FT. JACKSON, S.C.

So today I graduated and when I was standing there I was thinking about when Dennis told me how he hated the Army dress greens and I was thinking if he could only see this uniform. Then I realized he saw it before anyone else did. Miss you Dennis I know you didn't like the Army but I hope I'm a man in your eyes.

IT IS MY PRAYER . . .

When my journey ends and I meet you again face to face and hold you in my arms, as I begin to share with you each heart held moment that you missed since you left, I pray your only words to me will be, *"It is okay darlin', I know, I was with you the entire time."*

17748141R10156

Made in the USA
Middletown, DE
09 February 2015